The Girl
in the
Wicker Basket

The Girl in the Wicker Basket

ANN KENNY

WITH

YVONNE KINSELLA

EBURY
PRESS

1 3 5 7 9 10 8 6 4 2

Published in 2009 by Ebury Press, an imprint of Ebury Publishing
A Random House Group company
First published in Ireland by Poolbeg Press Ltd in 2008

The Random House Group Limited Reg. No. 954009

Addresses for companies within the Random House Group
can be found at www.randomhouse.co.uk

A CIP catalogue record for this book is available from the British Library

The Random House Group Limited supports The Forest Stewardship
Council (FSC), the leading international forest certification organisation.
All our titles that are printed on Greenpeace approved FSC certified paper
carry the FSC logo. Our paper procurement policy can be found at
www.rbooks.co.uk/environment

Printed in the UK by CPI Cox & Wyman, Reading, RG1 8EX

ISBN 9780091930127

To buy books by your favourite authors and register for offers visit
www.rbooks.co.uk

To my children

You are the light in my eyes

The hope in my heart

And the air that I breathe.

PROLOGUE

Changing Names

I wish I could tell you my real name and where I really grew up. And I wish I could show you some of the very few photos I have of my childhood; but unfortunately for me such things can never be. My whole life has been filled with lies and deceit. No one was ever honest with me. I grew up in a house of strangers and to them I was simply a slave; someone to clean for them, wash their clothes, cut wood for the fire and look after the animals.

When I decided to write this book, many years ago, I thought about what I should and shouldn't say. I debated whether I would actually name the members of the family who had taken every little piece of self-confidence from me, the people who had made me feel that I was absolutely worthless, that I didn't deserve to be loved. I spent so many nights worrying over how I could write my story without exposing the people who tried to destroy me, who beat me down at every opportunity.

I often asked myself: why should I protect them? Why shouldn't they pay for what they did to me? But after months, years of trying to come to terms with what actually happened to me as a child, as a teenager and even into my twenties, I decided that I wouldn't even give them the benefit of naming them, even if it was to shame them. I decided that this was going to be my story, not theirs – my words about my life.

All through my childhood and into my teens they let me know that to them I was nobody. The only names I was ever called were "bastard" or "you". But I never let them beat me down and I always told myself in later life that no matter what they said or did to me I was always Ann, and no one could take that away from me.

I was fostered and my name was changed, but unfortunately for me it took me years just to find that out and even longer to find out who I truly was. To explain everything and give you an idea of what my childhood was like, I have to go right back to the start. I have had no choice but to change places and names, but every single thing you are about to read is true – 100 per cent true. I have changed what I felt I had to change solely to protect my own children and everyone in my life who is special to me. But I have moved on and I now feel the time is right for me to tell my story. My Cinderella story, as my friends say.

JUST FOR ONE DAY

Let me be me – just for one day
To do what I want and go my own way
Just for one day let me not be your wife
Let me spread out my wings and make
some sense of my life
Just for one day let me not be your mother
Let me be whom I like and just lean on each other
Let me be the young child who got lost
through the years
Let me be sad for that child and let me shed a few tears
Let me be the teenager who got lost in the Sixties
With The Beatles, The Stones and the rest of the drifters
Let me not have the answers to the questions you ask
Let me be selfish and mean, let me dwell in the past
Don't let me be right if I want to be wrong
But do let me be weak 'cos I'm tired of being strong
Don't lean on my shoulder when you want to be sad
But let me lean on yours, or do you think that's bad?
So please when I ask you
Just for one day
Let me be what I want
And let me go my own way

CHAPTER ONE

A Ghost in my Head

A few years ago I asked my foster mother if there was ever another child in our house – a little girl who was kept in a wicker basket behind the door of the middle bedroom. For years I had a clear image of this little child just sitting there on her own, looking very lonely with no one paying any attention to her. Although I had never mentioned it to any of my family before, I was always intrigued as to whether it was a reality or just something that sprang from my over-active imagination.

This little girl was like a ghost in my head. I could see her as clear as day for as long as I could remember. This vision had stayed with me from when I was a young child, right up into my adult years. I had wrecked my head on so many occasions wondering if she was a relative, a cousin maybe, who came to stay with us for a while. Or maybe I had another sister who had died and whom I couldn't remember? But I had never asked.

My foster mother was a very hard woman. I had little or no relationship with her throughout my childhood. In fact, I don't think I ever had a child–mother chat with her at any time in my life. So just building up the courage to ask her this question was hard enough for me. Putting any question to my foster mother was always an ordeal. If she didn't like what I was asking, she would snap another question back at me, giving her time to get her thoughts together. I would feel like a little child all over again – even though at the time I was in my forties! Even as a child she would turn on me for absolutely no reason. The years had never mellowed her.

But I was curious to find out more about this little girl because I was convinced that she wasn't just a figment of my imagination. So when the opportunity arose and I finally put the question to her, she abruptly turned around, a big frown on her face, and bellowed, "Why do you want to know? What makes you think that there was a child in a basket?"

I decided not to let her get the better of me this time, so I braved it out and continued with my questioning. Part of me just wanted to leave before I infuriated her completely. I told her that I had no idea why I thought so often about this child, but that this vision had always been in my mind and it seemed very real. I explained that I could never understand where it came from, whether there was in fact a child or if I had simply dreamt it up.

She shifted herself back into the armchair uncomfortably and muttered, "Yes, there was a child in a basket and, yes, it was behind the door." She spoke so quietly that I had to strain to hear her reply. I was surprised by her answer. I thought she would say it was all in my mind. I expected her to belittle me, to have a laugh at my expense as usual. Also, even though in my head I could see this little child in a straw-type basket, I had led myself to believe all through my life that it probably *was* all in my mind. But it felt good that I appeared to be finally getting to the bottom of it. I was happy knowing that I wasn't going mad, that there *was* actually a child and a wicker basket – that it hadn't after all been an illusion.

I didn't have a normal childhood. I was treated very differently to all of my friends, although I didn't realise just how differently until many years later. And I was always made aware, especially by my mother, that I wasn't wanted. So I was intrigued by the fact that, for once, she was being honest with me. She wasn't leading me to believe that I was mad for a change.

Now that I was on a roll I really wanted to push her a bit more. I was dying to find out more. Dying to hear the full story. I was the youngest in the family, the baby so to speak, so if I could remember this little girl then she must have been the same age as me, or maybe just a year or two younger. Who was this child? When was she there? And why?

So much had happened in this old house and I had tried to block out so many of those thoughts and events of my childhood, that at times I didn't know whether certain things had actually taken place or whether I was just dreaming them up. So any scrap of background that I could find was manna from heaven for me. Every little morsel of information, no matter how tiny or unimportant it seemed to others, helped fill in that unfinished jigsaw bit by bit.

Unfortunately I went a step too far in asking too many questions at the same time and she became very agitated and angry. After much shouting she told me to mind my own business about things that didn't concern me.

Even as a child I always knew never to push this woman to the limit. If I did I would pay the price and I would remember it for the rest of my life. I had learnt from a very early age when to quit. So I sat back in the seat and just held my tongue. I made the decision to let it lie for a few days, to give her time to think about things and calm down; maybe then she would decide to fill me in and get it over with.

I knew there were so many things about my past that were covered up and I knew that, although my foster mother never liked me, she must have felt guilty at some stage in her life for making me feel so bad about myself. She had always treated me like a "nobody", so growing up I never knew where I fitted in. Somehow, I felt that I was always on the outside looking in. I had always hoped that some day she would just come clean with me about everything; not to help me – I knew that would never happen – but to make herself feel better. I prayed for it now more than ever, knowing that she wasn't getting any younger and that she might want to clear her conscience. I always clung onto this hope, but in my heart of hearts I knew miracles very rarely happened.

I was living in England at this time and I was over on one of my rare visits to the little village in Ireland where I grew up. I never liked going back there. But I made an effort every now and then to face my demons in the hope that things may have changed at home with this woman whom I called my mother. I always wondered if she would ever thaw out. Would she ever apologise to me for everything that had happened and would she ever forgive me for all the things that were blamed on me but which I never did? I think I also used to come back out of some kind of guilt. Guilt for what I don't know, but I always felt I owed her to come home every now and then. The truth was, I owed her nothing. She gave me nothing and I owed her nothing. But I came back anyway.

For this visit I had a few days to kill, as I had booked my plane ticket for a week and I had only arrived a couple of days earlier, so I thought I would just let her stew a bit. Before I headed home I would make it my business to solve the mystery of the girl in the wicker basket.

* * *

I spent the following days relaxing and planning my next move. I was staying in my friend Tricia's house, not too far from where my mother was living. It was great to be able to sit and chat in the evenings to someone who knew me so well. We have been best friends since childhood and we have always been there for each other, through thick and thin. When I told Tricia that my mother had confirmed that I wasn't losing my marbles and that there was indeed another child in the house who was kept in a wicker basket, even Tricia was confused. Tricia knew only too well of my past life and I had spoken about this dozens of times as we chatted over the years. Both us had always wondered what it was all about and who the child in the basket was.

A couple of days before I was due to head home to England I went back to my old home. This time I came bearing gifts, mainly cigarettes. I thought this might be a way to get on my mother's good side and soften her up a bit. She loved her drink as well but buying her alcohol was out of the question.

I remember thinking, as I walked up to the door for the second time that week, how funny it was that this place had never really changed over the years. It had aged and it needed some work done, but it was still the same as I remembered it as a child. The garden was overgrown and full of weeds, but the sort of TLC it needed was never something that came naturally here anyway, even when we were kids, so there was no change there.

When she opened the door I could see she wasn't happy that I was back. No matter when I visited over the years I rarely told her I would be there; I would just spring a surprise visit and wait for a reaction. I knew that if I did phone to say I was dropping over she wouldn't be staying in to bake a cake!

It was odd because this time I noticed how old she had got. It hadn't dawned on me before because I had been so distracted on my first visit that I didn't take as much in. But as I looked at her now, dressed in her cream jumper, white cardigan and black trousers with her glasses on and the usual frown on her forehead, she looked so much older than I remembered her. Her shoulders had started to droop and she just looked like an aged unhappier version of her previous self. It was clear that she was a very sad woman, with no one left in her life who cared for her or who she cared for. All of my family were dead except for herself and myself, and we weren't playing happy families.

She had been expecting me back, that was clear. She knew only too well that I was too stubborn to leave things as they were. After a minute or two she reluctantly walked back inside the house, ushering me in behind her. She gestured to me to sit down; no pleasantries exchanged. I wasn't offered a cup of tea – never was – and I dared not get up to make one because, as had been made clear to me all my life, it wasn't my home. When I settled in I gave her the cigarettes. I had bought her 200 Carrolls earlier in the day because I knew she wouldn't want a cake and I definitely wouldn't buy her flowers! She took the bag of cigarettes and sat down – no "thank you", nothing. I stood in the kitchen until she told me to sit down, because that's how it had always been in that house; I could never sit until I was told.

I started up a conversation. She was a very hard woman to chat to because I was never really comfortable, always watching my words and sitting on the edge of my seat. I watched for signs to see if she was defrosting a bit, watching her shoulders sinking slowly and her breathing relaxing. When I felt she had calmed down somewhat I approached the subject of the wicker basket again. The words weren't even out of my mouth when as quick as a flash she turned around on the chair.

"I knew you would be back. You always had a bloody nosy mind on you."

"That may be so, but I would still like to know who was in the basket."

She tensed up and her shoulders started to rise again.

"I suppose you are not going to leave until you know, are you?"

"I know that I can't force you to tell me, but yes, I would still like to know."

I couldn't understand what the big deal was. Why was she afraid to say who it was?

She took a deep breath and then sighed as she blurted out, "It was you, you bloody fool. And I thought you would have had the brains to work that one out for yourself. Who else did you think it was?"

I sat back into the chair and my chest felt like it had collapsed. For a minute I didn't know what to say or what to do. I was stunned. Somewhere in my mind I had always thought it was me; but if it was me, how could I have remembered it? More so, why would I remember it? Wicker baskets are fairly small; so if I were in this basket I would only have been a baby, probably three or four months at best, but the child I remember was definitely not a baby. And no matter how good a person's memory is, I think it would be virtually impossible for me to remember something that far back in my life.

There's no way I could remember when I was three months old. And even if it was me, and I was a new baby, why would it have left such an imprint in my mind? My mind was racing now and I wanted to find out more, to ask her all about it, but I knew I couldn't. There were a thousand questions racing through my mind and yet I was stuck. Stuck not knowing what to do next. I could see the smirk on her face and I knew by the way she was staring at me that she was daring me now to ask more. But I felt so confused now and she knew she had floored me. She knew I didn't expect her to say what she had just said. I was completely lost for words.

She continued to look at me with that evil, twisted face and said sarcastically, "Has the cat got your tongue? You wanted to know and I told you. Maybe you won't be so nosy the next time and will leave well enough alone."

It was the way she said things that made me feel sick. The way she stared at me with hatred in her eyes. She never had to tell me she hated me – it was more than obvious. All I wanted to do now was to get out of that house. I just wanted to run as quickly as possible, like I had many times before. I just wanted to get away from this woman because I knew that I would never find out why certain things happened to me and there was no point in tormenting myself anymore.

It had been hard going back on my own and I shouldn't have done it. It freaked me out just looking around the house as we had sat there. I remember wondering when had she replaced the fire with a Rayburn cooker, finding it odd that the old chair was still there, where it had always been and where he, father, had always sat. I remember as we talked trying not to stare out into the hall because every time I glanced out, from the corner of my eye I could see that little child standing there with her hands behind her back.

I wanted to ask her, "Why, why did you do everything you did to me over the years? Why did you treat me with utter contempt and yet always loved my two sisters?" But I couldn't find the words. I just turned my head away so I couldn't see out into that dark hall that held so many bad memories.

I knew she wanted me to leave anyway. I always knew when she wanted me to disappear and now, years later, in my adult years, I felt like a child again. Not wanted in that house. The house where I grew up unloved and despised for a reason I will probably never know. So I got up and went to the door and we said goodbye – no hugs, no kisses, just simply the word "goodbye" – and I left.

I was grateful for one thing, that I hadn't turned out like this woman, my so-called mother. I had three beautiful children of my own and every single day I told them that I loved them. They had all met their grandmother on a few occasions over the years but as expected she showed no more love to them than she had to me. She just treated them as if they were strangers in her home. No grandma hugs and kisses. No gifts for them when they arrived and none when they left. They were my children, the children of the child whom she had never wanted and to her they deserved no more love than she had given me.

On those previous visits I hadn't mentioned anything about my past because I didn't want any of the children to know how bad my childhood had been. It would have really hurt them to know the truth about my past and how I was treated growing up.

I had built myself up over the years for this day when I finally gathered the courage to question this woman, yet now I didn't know how I felt. It was as if I had finally opened a Pandora's Box but I still didn't really know what was in it. Earlier in the day as I drove to the house I had recited the Serenity Prayer to myself: "God grant me the serenity to accept the things I cannot change, courage to change the things I can and the wisdom to know the difference." And I kept saying it over and over in my head like a mantra to keep me strong. And I think it helped.

I had always wished that my foster mother could have been like my friends' mothers. I used to wonder why, if she didn't want me in the first place, she had taken me in at all. Don't foster mothers take children in to give them a new start in life, to help them rebuild their lives and to show them that somebody loves them? My whole life was confusing from the day I was born and she never did anything to change that. She never helped me understand why I was who I was. And she probably never would.

CHAPTER TWO

A House of Strangers

I would love to tell you that my birth was greeted with love and an overwhelming joy. I would love to say that in my mother's eyes, like all mothers, I was the most precious and the most beautiful baby in the world that she had ever seen. I would love to tell you this, but I can't. I can only tell you what I now know and that is that my birth was greeted with sheer relief from my mother, as she finally got rid of this thing that was growing inside of her for nine long months, and now, after giving birth to me, she could go back to whatever kind of life she was living before she had the misfortune of getting pregnant with a child she had never wanted.

My mother gave birth to me in the county home in a small country town in Ireland. There was a county home, I later found out, in nearly every county back in the fifties, places where unmarried mothers, who had "shamed" their families, were sent off to give birth in secret, so no one would find out how dirty and sinful they had been.

Most of these homes, including the one where I was born, were run by the nuns, who ruled these places with rods of steel. To say they did not think very highly of these unmarried mothers coming through their doors would be the understatement of the year. The way it worked was this: these young girls would arrive at the home thinking that they were going to be cared for, well-fed and clothed until they gave birth to their little bundles of joy. What they didn't know was that they had to pay for their keep from the time they unpacked their suitcases until they walked out of that place with empty arms and an empty womb.

As soon as they arrived and said goodbye to whatever family member had dumped them there, they were given a list of all the tasks they had to complete whilst they waited to deliver their bastard children, all conceived out of wedlock. They were forced to do all the domestic jobs around the home, no matter how sick or tired they felt, and the nuns probably saw it as a penance on earth for committing such a huge sin as having sex outside marriage. These poor young girls had to stay in these places either until someone came to collect them or until their little innocent babies, who had never chosen to come into this world, were adopted.

That is where and how my life began.

What happened to me immediately after my birth is still a bit of a mystery to me but it turned out that I was eventually raised just ten miles from the county home in a little village I will call Clara. This tiny one-horse town consisted in my time of just two sweet shops and two pubs. One of these pubs was also the local post office cum petrol station cum grocery store, and there was another little grocery store located just up the road from this multi-purpose building. There was also the tiny village school and the church.

Clara was typical of every other little village in Ireland at the time. It was a place where everyone knew everybody, and everybody knew everybody else's business. Nothing happened there that didn't go unnoticed. It was the type of place where very little of interest normally happened, so any little bit of juicy information or scandal was snatched up and spread about as quickly as possible. It was as if one person's misery was somebody else's amusement, although I guess that's the way things were and still are in a little village.

I was raised half a mile from the village by a family called the Nolans. The family consisted of my mother May (I call her my mother as she was the only mother figure I had), my father Mick and my two sisters, Nancy and Kate. We all lived in a three-bedroom council cottage situated right at the crossroads. The cottage was back from the road, and surrounded by high hedges and trees. It had a front lawn and the iron gate at the entrance was always padlocked. At the back of the house was a half-acre of land and various outhouses that my father used to hold the pigs and hens.

Mick Nolan was a tall thin man who worked with the local farmers, doing odd jobs and helping with the harvest. May, my mother, worked at painting and decorating people's houses. Kate and Nancy, their daughters, were like two little princesses, waited on hand and foot. They never had to lift a finger in the house and they were never chastised for doing anything wrong. They got away with murder.

And then there was me. They called me Rossie. I was the extra leg that never fitted in and I got into trouble for everything. It didn't matter if I hadn't done anything, I would pay the price as if I had. When you're a child you just accept things as they are. Children are brought up to respect their parents and never to question anything; isn't that how it has always been?

There were two old Irish sayings I remember hearing as a child. One was "Children should be seen and not heard". The other I would hear when I walked into a room when they, the family, were talking about something they didn't want me to hear. There would be a bit of a nod in my direction from one of them and then I would hear "Little pigs have big ears". I don't know why they bothered worrying about what I would hear because even if I did pick up something I shouldn't have heard I would have no one to tell it to. I was always a loner because I wasn't allowed to have friends. So in reality they had nothing to worry about.

There were rules in our house about how things were said and done but those rules were only for me. It's only when you get older and you think back on your childhood and the things that went on that you realise that what was actually happening wasn't normal. That's what I discovered when I began to trace my roots.

* * *

I find it very hard to put into words the way I was brought up and to write about the way other people treated me. Sometimes it seemed like I had leprosy or some other infectious disease. I was shunned by everyone, but I suppose what hurt me most was that I was shunned by my family. I honestly cannot remember my parents ever touching me, never mind hugging me.

The only bodily contact they ever had with me, as far as I can remember, was when I was getting a beating for something or other. And that would happen most days as I got older. There was a rule in the house, for me only of course, that I could only ever speak when I was spoken to. This is very, very difficult when you are a child. I wasn't allowed speak to my sisters, my mother or my father unless they addressed me. It was a very uncomfortable situation and I always wondered what I had done to make them treat me so badly. It's no wonder looking back now that I ended up with a stutter until I was sixteen.

As a child I grew up with the name Rossie. I had no reason to doubt that it was my name because that's what everyone called me, at home, in school and around the area. But years on I was to find out that I wasn't Rossie at all. It all came out when I found out that I was fostered. Seemingly, they refused to call me by my birth name so they just devised this name as a nickname for the area I came from, or rather from the birthplace of my mother.

From an early age Rossie was made to do all the dirty or difficult jobs around the place. This would consist of cleaning out the chicken house and feeding them; gathering sticks to light the fire in the morning; cleaning everyone's shoes, including Kate's and Nancy's. I also had to wash all the clothes, clear up and wash the dishes after every meal and be at their beck and call whenever they needed something done. I was a dogsbody. I was made only too aware of the fact that no one wanted me in the house and I was told constantly that I was a nobody, a good-for-nothing little bitch.

This was very hurtful to me because in my innocent little mind at the time I was one of their children and they were my mother and father. I would lie in bed most nights wondering, what have I done to make them all hate me so much? Why was I so different to Kate and Nancy? It was so upsetting for me.

* * *

The first beating that I remember happened when I was about four years old. I woke up one morning and realised that the bed was wet. I didn't remember doing it and it had never happened to me before, but I automatically felt guilty and blamed myself for what had happened. Kate was sleeping in bed with me this particular night but she didn't admit to anything when we woke up on the soaking wet sheets so I thought it had to have been me. I pleaded with Kate not to tell mother as I was scared stiff of what she would do to me. But she did and of course I paid the price.

I was standing in the bedroom on my own when I heard my mother shouting for me to come out to the kitchen. As I approached the kitchen from the hall, I started to shake. I was terrified in case she somehow knew what I had done. I saw her kneeling down at the fireplace, cleaning out the grate. When I got to the kitchen door she was putting ashes into a bucket with a shovel.

She shouted at me, "Get here." Sheepishly I went over and stood beside her. The next thing I remember is seeing her stand up and the shovel swing in her arm into the air as she hit me full force. The shovel connected with the side of my head and across my face.

Time seemed to stop and I went into shock. For a few seconds I felt completely numb. When I started to blink and come back to reality I suddenly felt something going pop around my eye. The next recollection I have is waking up lying on my back on the floor in the hallway. I felt something cold running down my face and into my mouth. My face hurt so much. I put my hand up to touch it. I could feel a big lump around my eye. As I took my hand down from my face I noticed it was soaked in blood. I was too scared to cry in case she would come and beat me again.

I don't know how long I lay there, but I was too frightened to get up until I was told, and nobody came to see if I was all right. I must have drifted in and out of sleep for some time, because what I remember next is them coming in the front door, laughing and chatting. I realised that they had all been to Mass and they had left me lying on the cold floor in the hallway.

My first thought was that I had missed Mass. I liked going to Mass. I used to feel that going to the church was like having a day out. It got me out of that house for a while so I loved going to the church and seeing all the locals gathered outside afterwards, chatting away. At the time I didn't think it was odd that my family had just gone off and left me covered in blood and unconscious on the floor. In my little child's head, I had been bold and I had just been punished for that and unfortunately that's what happens when you're bold.

I don't remember any of them coming to see if I was okay, but I do recall my mother shouting from the kitchen, "Rossie, are you going to lie there all day? You had better get up before your father sees you." I must have had some sort of concussion because I don't know what happened next. I probably just got up and got on with what I had to do. If I hadn't, God only knows what would have happened then and I would have remembered it. The only other thing I recall about that time is that I didn't go to school for a few days after my "accident". I must have looked a sight – I had a big black eye and quite a few marks on the side of my face.

* * *

A few months later mother had to take me to an eye clinic in the nearest large town. I must have been having problems seeing. Maybe she was feeling a bit guilty and noticed how my sight seemed to be deteriorating, as I was always bumping into things. It must have got fairly bad for her to even think about bringing me to see someone. It was very rare for me to even go to a doctor; I think I would have had to be at death's door for her to take me to a GP.

In the clinic they asked her if I had injured my eye. She told them that I had run into a wall while I was playing and bashed my head. I remember those words as clear as day. I sat there listening to her lying outright. They told her that I had lost most of the vision in my left eye, and they were surprised that I had not been seen to when I had *supposedly* run into the wall. I always thought it was odd that they had never investigated it further, considering the massive amount of damage done to my eye.

My visits to that clinic lasted for years. I would attend two or three times a year and they would put drops in my eyes that would make me practically blind for most of the day. Afterwards mother would take me into the local Woolworths, as she would be buying something for her two "lovely" daughters. I always desperately wanted to look at the toys, but I couldn't see them as my vision was very blurred.

On the way to the clinic one day I asked mother if she would take me to Woolworths first, before I got the drops in my eyes. She asked me why I wanted to go before the clinic and I said I would be able to see all the toys in Woolworths if we went beforehand, as I couldn't see them afterwards. She said that I didn't deserve to see anything after all the trouble I had caused.

I never did get to see the toys.

* * *

In the morning times when I got up I would come into the kitchen for breakfast. It was the same routine every day. I would be handed a bowl of what I now know was gruel, a kind of porridge-type substance. It was absolutely rotten, thick and tasteless, but if I didn't eat it I would have to starve for the day, so I had no choice really. I remember that mother would cook another breakfast for everyone else, a steamed porridge dish with sugar and sometimes cream, but I was obviously not good enough to have the tastier stuff. On the days when she ran out of gruel, or she didn't have time to cook it, I would have bread and margarine.

I was never allowed to sit at the table to eat with the rest of the family. It just never happened. I would watch from the bedroom or the hall as they all sat down at the table that I had laid for them. I would often wish I could join in and have a chat, like every other family. But mealtimes, more than any other time, proved to me how much I was really despised. As they sat around laughing and joking and talking about the things that every normal family laugh and joke about, I was left to eat alone, every single day of every single week, from about the age of four. When people came to the house visiting I never got to see them, nor did they see me. To this day I still don't know why the family were so ashamed of me, or embarrassed by me.

These were very quiet and lonely times for me. As soon as I had finished the morsels I was given to eat I would have to go straight back out again to work on the land. I used to try to prolong the time in the house, eating my bread and margarine, just so that I could stay warm for a little longer, or for whatever reason would be going through my head at the time.

To this day I can never stomach having margarine in the house. Even if I am baking a cake and I need to use margarine, I will buy something similar instead, as the smell of it still turns my stomach.

Apart from mealtimes or when I was doing chores, I was never allowed in the house during the day. In the warm weather I would have to stay in the back garden. I would gather twigs from around the garden to make dolls and I used to dress them up with leaves and lay them down in their beds, which I made out of straw. I used to play imaginary games with them and tell them all about everything that had happened to me.

In winter I was locked in the shed. They were probably afraid I'd get sick if I was left outside and they'd have to pay for a doctor. The shed was concrete and attached to the side of the house. It was used to keep some of the animals. It was bitterly cold in there so I would huddle up in a ball in a corner to try and keep the heat in. They wouldn't even leave a blanket on the floor for me and there was nothing for me to amuse myself with, except the hens, so I would just sit there, sometimes shaking with the cold.

When it was time to come into the house at night, or to do some chores, I was made to stand in the hallway with my hands behind my back and wait there until I was called into the kitchen. This I found very hard to do because I had to stand dead still if I wanted to be allowed in. I used to be so desperate to look into the kitchen, just to see what they were all doing, as I could hear all the talking and laughing.

To distract my mind, I used to count the patterns, flowers or dots on the wallpaper. It was at times like this that I would rather have been out in the shed with the animals. I felt as though the hens and the pigs were my only friends.

* * *

My father was a very hard man. He made me work from morning till night, no matter what kind of weather we had. From a very young age I would have to cut big heavy logs with him with a two-handled saw. He would hold one end and I would hold the other, and we would pull it backwards and forwards. I used to end up with cuts and blisters all over my hands from where he would have pulled the saw so fast and so hard that my knuckles would bash into the log. He would see the blood running down my fingers but he wouldn't stop. In fact he would pull it even harder, just to see if I would cry, for if I cried he would either hit me or throw the log at me, and tell me that I was good for nothing.

Father also helped the local farmers out by working with them in the fields every year thinning out the sugar beet. These fields were huge and could have been anything from half a mile to a mile long. All of this work was done manually on the hands and knees in the fields and father used to get me up at five in the morning to go and help him. I would have to work with him until about half past seven. Then I would have to walk home on my own, feed the hens, clean out the pigs, bring firewood into the house – all before I had anything to eat.

I would then wash, change my clothes, have my usual bowl of gruel and go to school. And I would repeat the same procedure all over again when I got home. My knees and back used to kill me and I never got a penny for all I did. I did this every year from the age of nine until I was about sixteen. I could never understand why Kate and Nancy didn't have to do it. I suppose it would have been too much like hard work for his precious daughters, who never did anything anyway. They were too good to be seen down on their hands and knees doing manual labour.

To be fair to him, my father wasn't as bad as mother, but sometimes he could be very cruel to me and there were times when he broke my heart. Once I had a teddy bear – I have no idea where it came from, or who gave it to me, but I know I loved him. He was tatty, old and had one eye, but he was everything to me and I adored him with all my little heart. They all knew I idolised teddy and how I hated even leaving him at home when I went to school. I used to talk to him all the time as well because I didn't have anyone else to talk to, so teddy knew all my problems.

One day I came home from school and as usual went into the bedroom to change out of the best of the hand-me-down clothes I wore to school to the worst of the hand-me-downs I wore to do my chores. I had my own little routine – I would slip teddy into my knickers when I was putting on my working clothes, so they wouldn't see him and grab him from me, and then I would take him outside with me so that I could tell him about my day at school. However, this particular day when I took off my school clothes, I went to get teddy but he was nowhere to be seen. I always left him in the same place so I couldn't understand where he could have gone. I looked everywhere for him but I couldn't find him.

Out of the corner of my eye, as I was pulling everything around, I noticed my father standing at the bedroom door watching me. He asked what I was doing and I said, "Looking for my teddy."

I will never forget or forgive him for what he said next.

He looked at me with contempt and mumbled, "Oh, that old thing. I decided today that you were too old for all that carry-on so I threw him in the fire."

I was eight and a half years old and he thought I was too old for a teddy bear. I could have died there on the spot. I swallowed the lump that was rising in my throat and held back the tears until I got outside. I felt lost. I would never see teddy again. What would I do? Who could I talk to? I couldn't believe he could do that to me. I didn't have anything else in my life, no friends, no toys and no family. Why would he take teddy from me? I couldn't understand it and that day he really did break my heart.

* * *

On another occasion he brought home a lamb that was born in the fields with a broken back. The poor little thing was tiny and so cute. He said that he was going to kill it in the morning. I couldn't believe he would do that to a poor little furry lamb that could harm no one. The poor little thing had already been taken from his mother and now he was going to kill him. I cried my eyes out when I heard what he was going to do. I even got down on my knees in the kitchen and I begged him not to kill it. I promised that I would look after it and it wouldn't cause any trouble. I would make sure it was okay.

He turned to me with a sneer on his face and sarcastically said, "You – look after this?" And I just innocently said, "Yes." I told him that he need never worry about it and I promised that I would do extra work if he let me keep the lamb.

I didn't know what extra work I could do, because I was doing everything in and out of the house as it was, but I knew he would find something for me. For weeks and months I took great care of this little sick lamb. To be fair to father, he did build a swing in the shed to enable him to stand unaided. I would take this little animal, whom I called Fluffy, out to graze in the field and hold him between my legs so that he would be able to stand up. I would clean up after him every morning and evening along with all the work I had to do.

It didn't take long for Fluffy to grow big and he seemed to be getting stronger every day. And I loved watching him do different things for himself as the weeks and months went on. It was like I was his mammy, because I was the only one who cared for him and made sure he was fed and loved.

Then one afternoon I came home from school and Fluffy was gone. No explanation, nothing. I looked everywhere for him but I knew I would never find him. I was too afraid to ask what had happened, so I said nothing. I wasn't stupid. It was fairly obvious. Father simply told me to go and clean the shed. He never said anything about the lamb going missing. He acted as if the fluffy white lamb had never even been there. He knew how I had nursed him and loved him and he still got rid of him.

But I never cried in front of him, as that would have shown my father my weakness. I cried on my own, in the shed, as I cleaned up all the dirt. I cried and cried and before I went back inside that house I made sure that I showed no signs of being upset. I wouldn't give them that satisfaction. I knew they were looking for signs to see if I was upset but

I never gave them any reason to think it. But for two whole weeks I never spoke to any one of them. I took all the wallops and beatings that they dished out to me as usual, and got on with whatever I had to do. I remember thinking that I would never again care for anything or anyone. No matter what I had, it was always taken from me.

* * *

My relationship with Kate and Nancy simply did not exist. Kate was about seven years older than I was and Nancy was about five years older.

You would think that they would have loved to take care of their little sister, look after her and make sure that nothing ever happened to her, but they never liked me. I was only ever good for doing things for them, cleaning their shoes, sorting their clothes and cleaning up after them. In all the years I lived with them they never showed any signs that they cared at all. I have tried to think what these two girls were like, but I can't think of anything that stood out in them that would make me say, "Yes, they were good and kind to me." They hardly ever spoke to me. If they did, it would only be to tell me to get something or to do something. It's terrible to say that I have very little knowledge of my sisters. I wouldn't even know what colour their eyes were, what way they wore their hair, what kind of music they liked . . . nothing.

I could say the same of mother and father; I knew nothing about them either. I lived in a house of strangers.

* * *

One time when father was in hospital and I was about nine years old Nancy went out to the back garden to try to chop some wood with father's axe. She didn't have a clue what to do because she had never done it before. She couldn't get the log to stand up for her so she asked me to hold it steady. I was feeling a bit bitchy and refused do it because I still had loads of jobs to finish myself. My mother opened the window and shouted at me, "You do what Nancy tells you to do or you get no supper." So I did as I was told and held the log for Nancy.

The axe came down. Not only did it split the log but it almost sliced my finger off as well.

There was blood rushing everywhere and Nancy ran into the house screaming. I was left sitting on the ground out the back yard holding my hand in the air as the blood dripped down onto the ground and all I could hear was mother shouting and screaming. I don't know what she was saying or to whom, but I do know I was the last person to get attention, even though the top of my finger was hanging off.

Eventually mother came out into the back yard and she dragged me inside and put my hand in a basin of freezing cold water to wash off the blood, which was still pouring out. She then tore up an old sheet, wrapped it around my hand and told me that it was okay. The blood was seeping through non-stop but there was no doctor, no stitches, nothing. It took months for my finger to heal. To this day I still have the scar.

Nancy never apologised or even asked if I was okay. And I didn't get a break from doing any of the chores. Things went on as usual, finger or no finger.

* * *

Kate and Nancy had the best of everything while I on the other hand had nothing. My sisters of course were spoilt rotten – new clothes, new shoes, new toys – while I always had the hand-me-downs, even if they were too big for me. The worst of the hand-me-downs were the wellington boots, as they were always hanging off me and they used to leave my shins red raw from where they would have rubbed off the skin.

I always envied the girls when I saw their new clothes. Every summer mother used to take them into the big city nearby and they would come home with bags of new t-shirts, flowery dresses and shoes. She did the same in the winter, when they got new boots and winter coats. I don't remember ever getting anything new from my family. My new clothes were just their old clothes, the ones that were showing signs of wear and tear, the ones that were going out of fashion and the ones that were too small for them (but often too big for me). It was only years later that I learned that the money she was spending to buy her two daughters clothes was actually meant to be for me, the money for fostering me. I learned also that she was given a fairly big allowance twice a year for me from the government to get me whatever I needed. But I never saw anything from it.

The only time that I can remember wearing anything

that I think was new was on my Confirmation Day. I can't remember my First Holy Communion, as there weren't any photographs taken that I can recall. However, I do remember my Confirmation Day, but not for any of the reasons you're supposed to remember this day for. I should remember it for making my vows to love God and not to drink alcohol, or for meeting the Bishop, or even for the name that I took, a name I can't even remember.

What I do remember about my Confirmation Day is my gorgeous deep red coat. It was the most beautiful thing that I had ever seen. Where it came from I do not know. I always convinced myself that they had bought it especially for me for that day to make me feel special. I know that would have been a miracle, but it's nice to think that at some stage in their lives they bought me something special. This wonderful coat had a lovely black velvet collar and black buttons down the front. I felt like a little princess in it. Sadly, my one and only positive experience of this occasion was short-lived, for after the Confirmation Day I never saw the coat again. It just disappeared overnight, but I have never forgotten it.

THE MEANING OF FEAR

F is for Fear that I have every day
E is for Emotions that won't go away
A is for Always at the forefront of my mind
R is for Reasons that I try so hard to find

CHAPTER THREE

Grandfather

I have no recollection of when grandfather came to live with us. But as I try to put the pieces of this big puzzle together, I am guessing that I must have been only three or four years old at the time. Johnny, my grandfather, was my foster-mother's dad. I have no idea what I called him, but I know that if he were able to speak from the grave he would remember only too well what he called me. I had a number of names ranging from "a little bastard" to "a good-for-nothing piece of shit". He was never short of degrading names for his youngest granddaughter. He was a tall man, with a head of grey hair. The most memorable thing about him was that he always had sweets in his pockets. Of course, I never got to taste many of them; he gave most of them to his other granddaughters to enjoy.

I felt very frightened and uneasy when I was with him, as

he would lash out at me for the slightest thing. It wouldn't have been unusual for me to wet my knickers when he was around, as he liked to knock me flying with a sudden slap across the face on a regular basis. There would be no warning sign; one minute I'd be standing there innocently and the next thing I'd be on the floor with a stinging pain right across my face. Once again, I don't know why he did that. I think he just liked to show his authority.

One day in school, when I was about six years old, I started to pull at a loose piece of wool on the green school jumper that my mother had knitted for one of the girls and then handed down to me. I was a bit bored and I started twiddling with this little bit of wool as I listened to what was being said in class. Suddenly I looked down and noticed that I had the whole middle ripped out of the jumper. All that was left was the ribbed end and part of the chest and the two arms, each part hanging onto the other by a bit of wool.

It was the last class and when school was over I headed home, absolutely terrified about what would happen when mother saw what I had done. I knew that she would see it as a mortal sin and I would pay dearly for my crime. As I walked in the door her face said it all. She started to scream at me, asking what the hell I had done to the jumper. She was ranting and raving, flinging her arms in the air. She kept shouting at me, telling me that I was an ungrateful bitch and I didn't deserve to have anything. I got the lecture about my two sisters never doing anything like this and how I should have been ashamed of myself. I got a good beating from her that evening which left me in agony for the rest of the night. She was always careful not to leave any tell-tale signs when she beat me, no marks on my face or anything. She would carefully plant every wallop in a place where she knew no one could see it. I had grown to accept that this was just how my life was going to be and there was no point in complaining. No one would listen anyway.

Later that evening, just before tea, I was standing at the kitchen table, waiting on my food, when grandfather casually stood up from his chair, walked over to the table, grabbed me by the ear, dragged me to the middle of the floor and ordered me to take off all my clothes. Mother was sitting beside the fire and Kate and Nancy were sitting on the other side of the fireplace, nice and cosy. Not one of them batted an eyelid. I remember feeling absolutely terrified. I was trembling with fear because I didn't know what he was going to do. I stripped as I had been told to do and stood there naked, trying to cover myself with my hands. With that he took the belt off his trousers, staring me straight in the eye. He looked as though he had been possessed by the devil. He could see that I was shaking with fear and I knew when I saw the belt come off what was going to happen. My clothes had fallen to the floor at my feet and I held my knees close together to stop myself from shaking so much.

With that he started to beat me viciously from head to toe with the hard leather belt. I looked over at my foster-mother with pleading eyes, begging her to save me, but she did nothing. As he continued with the beating he kept shouting, "I'll beat the bloody badness out of you, you stubborn little bastard, see if I don't. You'll be sorry you were ever born before I'm through with you."

As the belt came down on me time after time, I

wondered what I had done to deserve this. It couldn't be just because a thread was loose on the jumper and it fell apart. Why was he saying I was filled with badness? Yet again I was getting beaten to a pulp and being called all sorts of terrible names and l couldn't understand why it was happening. The pain of the belt coming down on my skin was unreal. The sting shot through me every time he made contact with my little frame. But from the start I told myself that I wasn't going to cry. I wasn't going to give him the satisfaction of seeing he was hurting me. But it was very hard to do because the beatings just went on and on.

I focused on telling myself over and over again that this was not hurting me. I saw him stare with disgust at my emotionless face and I knew it was to get worse. Seeing that his efforts were in vain he decided to beat me even harder, using the buckle this time. I quietly prayed that he would run out of steam and stop. Then I felt and tasted blood running down my face and into my mouth. I knew that he had hurt my head badly as he was lashing me from top to bottom. I could see that with every whipping he gave me the girls were jumping. Even the noise of the lashings terrified them and yet my mother allowed them to sit there and watch me take this beating.

When I tasted the blood it was as if all the pain hit at once. I couldn't hold it in any longer. I let it all out and screamed for him to stop. Try as I did to stop them, the tears came rolling down my face, mixing with the blood and dropping onto the kitchen floor.

When he saw that he had finally beaten me I heard him say to mother, "See, I told you I'd beat it out of her." With that he casually looped the belt back onto his trousers, sat down in the chair and lit up his pipe. In his head, I suppose, it was a job well done. My mother, who had sat through it all as a spectator, casually told me to go outside and wash myself, as the blood was all over her floor.

Naked, bleeding and aching with pain, I had to make my way outside in the cold to wash the blood from my torn and scarred skin. When I eventually came back in she told me to go straight to bed and not to say a word. As I lay in the bed, feeling lonelier than I had done in a long time, I sobbed and sobbed. It wasn't because I was hurting all over, nor was I crying because I was sad, lonely and scared. No; I cried because I was hungry. Absolutely starving. I had been sent to bed without any supper and hadn't eaten a thing since early that morning when I'd had a bowl of mother's special gruel. I knew they would not bring me anything so I would have to go to sleep weak with pain and hunger pangs. To make it worse, I could hear them all in the kitchen, laughing and talking. And I just had to lie there on blood-stained sheets and try my best to block out the noise.

* * *

Grandfather seemed to take out all of his frustrations on me, using me as his whipping dog. He never laid a finger on the other girls. And he was not just physically cruel. The man was equally as vicious with his weird mind games.

One time, when I was about six or seven, he took me down to the village as he was going to the pub to have a few pints, which was something he liked to do a lot. We walked

down the old country road; it was about fifteen minutes'
walk to the pub but before he went into the local he called
into the sweet shop and bought two chocolate pies. These
pies looked like ice cream wafer cones filled with a fluffy
creamy mousse and then covered in milk chocolate. They
were delicious, a real treat for a child. He said he was buying
them for Nancy and Kate; nothing for me. I was told to sit
on the window ledge outside the pub and hold these two
cones in this bag and wait for him to finish his drink. He told
me that on no condition was I to touch them.

Now that's a very difficult thing for a child to do. It
would be like putting a bowl of cream down for a cat and
telling him not to drink it. I sat on that window ledge with
a longing just to lick one of these cones, but I knew that if I
did I would get the mother of all beatings. However, the
longer he stayed in the pub the worse the temptation
became. I thought to myself, sure I'm beaten by one of them
most nights for something or other and I've had bad ones
before, so having a bite of one of these would make up for
what I would get when I went home. I never got sweets from
my parents or from grandfather – unless I had done
something special for him, something that would remain a
secret between him and me – so I thought I'd just go for it
and pay the price later. I decided to play it safe and not eat
the whole cone, just taste it. So I took the chocolate very
carefully off the top of the cone, scooped out all the cream
inside and wolfed it down. It tasted delicious. I did this to
both of them and then I carefully put the chocolate back on
top of the cones and put them back in the bag.

On the way home, after he'd had a few drinks inside him,

he told me that if I was a good girl for him I would be able to eat them both! So I promised I'd be good. Being good normally meant that I would sleep with him that night. I agreed.

I slept with grandfather a lot as a child. Just him and me huddled together in the bed. It was the only time of the day when he would show me affection, give me hugs and kiss my neck. But I never realised until later in my life just how affectionate he actually was on those nights. It took many years for me to remember what happened on those dark evenings but as a child I just accepted whatever was to be.

On that particular day when we got back to the house, after me promising to be a good girl again, he simply handed me the bag back and said I could have them both for myself but not to tell the girls.

These were the sort of games my grandfather would play with me on a regular basis. No "hide 'n' seek", no card games like Snap and no innocent grandfather hugs. He played with the other two all right, his favourite girls as he liked to call them, and I was forced to look on in envy.

* * *

I was eight when grandfather died, a day that has been imprinted in my mind forever. It's amazing that an eight-year-old can actually remember the time someone died. It was around midday on Tuesday, the 16th of September 1958. When I heard he had died I didn't know whether to laugh, sing, or dance; all I knew was that I wasn't going to, nor did I want to, cry.

I was at school when the Master came into Miss Byrne's classroom. I was standing in the corner at the very end of the classroom with the other children. I saw him look down at me and I knew before he even said anything that I was going to be going home. The Master didn't come into the class looking for a child unless they had to go home for some reason, that was just the way. He called my name and said that Kate and Nancy were waiting outside for me and that I was to go home with them. He told us that there was some bad news and that grandfather had died.

The girls were all tearful and hugging each other, but neither of them said or did anything to me. I was just numb. No feelings whatsoever, except relief to think that my body would hopefully never hurt again. They were chatting amongst themselves but never spoke to me at all on the way home. When we eventually got to the house Nancy and Kate ran into the hall crying for their mother. I was stopped at the door and told I was not allowed in and that I was going away to stay with neighbours who lived over two miles away. I asked my foster mother if I could see grandfather. She snapped at me, "No!" Then she turned to face me, having released her grip on Nancy and Kate, and said, "Get out of here and don't come back until you are told."

The family I was to stay with were at the house and they took me off with them in their car. I didn't even know them to talk to, just to see every now and then, but it didn't bother any of them that I was being sent off into the dark on my own with virtual strangers.

I was sent up to bed when we got in but later that night

I woke up and the house was very dark and scary. I couldn't find anyone around so I got dressed, left the house and walked the whole two miles back to my own house in pitch-black darkness. I was only eight years of age. When I eventually got to our house there were lots of people there, so I walked straight into the bedroom where grandfather was lying dead in the bed. I heard someone shouting to my mother, "Oh my God, Rossie is here, she is in the bedroom." My mother jumped up and started screaming, "Get her out of here." It was like something you would see in a mad house. I have no idea why they were shouting at me, because all I wanted was to see for myself that he really was dead. If he was dead, he wasn't going to hurt me any more, was he? And I couldn't understand why my sisters were allowed in and everyone was feeling sorry for them while I was being thrown out like a dirty animal. However, they let me stay on in the house that night after all the fuss.

Two days later, on the day he was going to be buried, I was in the bedroom and I could hear that there were a lot of people around, in the kitchen and the sitting area. My foster mother stormed into the bedroom and grabbed me by the arm and out into the hallway where grandfather was lying in his coffin. The lid had not been put on yet and I could see he was dressed in his good suit. I remember wondering if he had any sweets left in his pockets.

Someone was holding a saucer with holy water on it and a sprig of hedge. My foster mother told me to pick up the sprig and to shake the holy water over him and while I was doing it I was to tell him that I was sorry for being a bad girl. I couldn't remember being bad and I turned to my mother and said, "But I wasn't a bad girl." Within seconds she had turned right around and walloped me full force across the face. In front of everyone she said that he was only dead because of me. I had no idea what I had done wrong, but I said sorry to him rather than get another wallop. Once that was done and I had apologised to the man who made my life hell in many ways, they put the lid on his coffin and took him away.

Forever.

CHAPTER FOUR

Schooldays

The day after the funeral it was back to school as usual for me. Although the family was in mourning and the girls were allowed to stay at home I was secretly delighted to be able to get on with life without the fear of what that man would do to me when I got home or when I went to bed at night. I was delighted to be back at school so soon and back to a bit of normality surrounded by other kids.

The school was in the centre of the village. It was an old building with just two classrooms, one for the infants or juniors who were aged between four and ten years of age and the other for what they called the masters, who were aged ten to thirteen. There was a playground on both sides of the building, one for the boys and one for the girls. Under no circumstances were we allowed to mix while we were in the playground; your life would not have been worth living if you were caught even looking in at the boys.

The toilets for the children were situated outside; they looked like big holes dug from the ground with planks of wood sitting on top with large circles cut out of the top. When I was small it was very hard to sit on them, and I was always afraid that I would fall down into the hole, into God knows what. There were also two big water tanks at the back of this building, which must have been used for drinking water and probably bathroom water as well. Wherever the water came from, it tasted horrible and was definitely not hygienic.

Inside the school, the two rooms were divided by a partition. This was pulled back every now and then when the whole school would have to come together for an event like assembly, or when only one of the teachers was in. We only had two teachers, Miss Byrne, who taught the infants and juniors, and Master Dunphy, who taught the older kids. To my mind, Miss Byrne seemed pretty old – I'm not sure exactly how old because when you're a child everyone seems old – but she was definitely at least fifty. She used to drive a black Morris Minor car and every morning when she parked the car outside the school one of the children would come over and open the school door for her and she would then tell us all to get in line. She may have been in the class for a good ten or fifteen minutes but no matter what the weather was like we would have to wait outside until she decided to call us into the classroom. She liked to show that she was in control.

One thing that stands out about Miss Byrne is that, in the

cold weather when the fire was lit in the classroom, she would walk over to it, pull up her skirt and warm her backside. Her knickers – I suppose they would be called bloomers – were the biggest I had ever seen; they came down to her knees.

As a teacher she was a bit odd because she had a few personalities. Her humour would change from one minute to another, never mind every day. Sometimes she was very strict and at other times she was really fair with us. Once in class she asked us to spell "porridge"; I was the only one who got it right so she gave me a three-pence piece, which was a lot for a child back then. On another occasion, when she asked me to recite the Creed – "I believe in One God, the Father Almighty, Maker of Heaven and Earth" – not a word came out of my mouth. Although I knew it off by heart, I could not say the words. I had a very bad stammer and at times I just froze. She knew this but she still made me stand with my face against the wall for the whole day. Apart from these few things, I did like Miss Byrne – which is more than I can say about Master Dunphy.

Master Paul Dunphy was a different kettle of fish. This is how we discovered his name was Paul. One day in the yard we were reciting the nursery rhyme, "Two little dickie birds sitting on a wall, one named Peter, the other named Paul". Master Dunphy came out of the school and told us not to play that game again; if we did we would get the strap. We found out later that he had a brother called Peter; and yes, he did have a strap in the classroom that he used on numerous occasions. The master was tall, slim, bald, and rode a bike. He lived in the same town as Miss Byrne, but they never came to school together. I always got the feeling that they didn't like each other, as they hardly ever spoke in school.

He came from the west of Ireland but I don't know how he came to teach in our little village. We were always told to call him the master, and it suited him because he ruled over his pupils with a rod of steel. However, if you came from a wealthy farm family, or you happened to be a shopkeeper's son or daughter, you were blessed because he would not dare harm a hair on your head for fear of being reported to the school board. For those of us less fortunate, he used anything that came to hand when he wanted to hit us, from canes to straps to belts.

* * *

Despite these little "hiccups", I did like school. Maybe it was because it was time spent away from home and I could be around normal children. There was one downside to being with the other kids though – hardly any of them would play with me. I don't know why. Back then I used to think it was because I stuttered so badly and they couldn't be bothered with me, but it could have had something to do with my older sisters telling stories about me. I couldn't change that so I just had to live with it. It never put me off school though.

When I was about nine years old someone in the school playground called me a bastard. I remember everyone laughing but I had no idea what the word meant, although I had been called it many times at home. When mother used this word to me I just took it to mean I was a bad girl; but hearing other kids calling me this made me realise that it meant more. I was upset that they were calling me names but I didn't have a clue why. So when I got home that day after school I asked my mother what a bastard was, and the answer came by way of a hard wallop across the face. So I was none the wiser as to the meaning of the word, which meant I couldn't fight back when I was called it again. And after the first girl kick-started the word, it stuck and I would be slagged on a regular basis.

Because of the way I was treated both at home and at school, I often thought that there must have been something wrong with me. No matter how hard I tried to be good or do my work I was never picked for anything in school. Even on sports days I was always left standing on the sideline. It was the same in the playground – the girls would never come and pick me to join in their games, so I would wander around the yard on my own. Sometimes I would go into the field where the boys were playing hurling and I'd step in as their goalkeeper. However, I took a big chance doing this as the girls were not allowed to play with the boys. If I had been caught there would have been hell to pay. The lads didn't seem to mind me being in goal and once I was inside the net, the teachers couldn't see if they looked out the windows.

It wasn't only in school that I was shunned – very few people spoke to me. Looking back, though, I hardly saw anyone to speak to. On the odd occasion when they'd let me go to the local shop for groceries, I was always given a note. So even the shopkeeper had no reason to speak to me and would just hand over the groceries.

Now, I was not the perfect pupil, nor did I take everything that was dished out to me lying down, even if it did mean getting into trouble in school and at home. At times I walked myself into things with the master. He had his favourites and it was important that we other kids found out early just who these favourites were to save ourselves unnecessary trouble. If you got on well with these "special" kids you had a better chance of survival.

The master had a habit of looking in the window of the classroom before he came in but on one of these mornings I didn't notice him staring in as I was too busy reading a card that my mother had filled in giving permission to allow me to go with the other children to have some x-rays taken in the afternoon. These health checks were just a routine thing in every school. The master walked into the room, made his way up behind me and tapped me on the shoulder, pointing to the top of the classroom. When you are told to go to the top of the classroom, you know you are in trouble. I walked sheepishly to the top of the room wondering what I had done. I saw him reach for the stick and before he had a chance to whack me I quickly asked him what I had done wrong.

He said very crossly, "You were talking and messing around."

"It wasn't me, sir, it was the two girls in front of me."

Stupid mistake – because the two in front were a farmer's daughter and the local shopkeeper's daughter.

Needless to say he didn't listen. He gripped my right wrist tightly so that there was no way I could move my hand away. He gave me two hard wallops on the right hand. He then went to hit me on the left hand and I said to him, "You can't hit me on this hand, sir, as it will only bleed."

This was the hand that Nancy had sliced with the axe, which had taken months to heal because of my mother's negligence. On most days I would use it as an excuse so that he wouldn't hit me again. The master was not having any of my nonsense on this particular morning and told me that he was sick of me using that excuse, so he promptly gave me two more wallops on the sore hand. I quietly returned to my seat.

By now it was time to kneel and say morning prayers. The pain was piercing through my hand but I tried not to think about it and concentrated on my prayers. During the course of the chants, the wound in my finger started to open up and began bleeding badly. Anne Walshe, who was kneeling beside me, could see what was happening as I was trying to stop the blood from getting onto my clothes, in case I got into trouble at home. When prayers were finished Anne said, "You had better tell him." I told her I couldn't because I felt it would only cause more trouble for me if I said anything. With that the master shouted down to Anne asking what was going on and why she was talking. She said, "Master, Rossie's hand is bleeding badly." He called me to the desk and told me to show him my hand. The blood was still running from it and he took me outside to wash myself and put something on to cover it and stop the bleeding.

Before I went home that day, he gave me a half crown and told me not to tell anyone that he had hit me on my bad finger. Needless to say I went home and told my mother, only for her to respond that I must have deserved it. No pity there.

* * *

On another occasion, I was sent out to the green area near the school to find a stick for the master as he had broken most of the ones he had and wanted some more. It wasn't unusual for him to send one of the pupils out to find sticks for him to hit us with. I set off happily to find a stick, knowing that at least I was getting out of class for a while. I got one that was a bit thick at the top end and very thin at the bottom, and when you shook it, it went *whish*. It was what we called a sally switch. When you got hit with it the thin bit would wrap around your fingers.

I must have had a wicked mind because I remember thinking that whoever got hit with this one would remember it. I came back into the classroom with the stick, smiling happily to myself, thinking he was going to be pleased with me for choosing a good strong one.

I handed him the sally switch and he asked me to wait for a minute, as he was busy doing something. I stood there hoping I was going to get either a sweet or some other reward. What I got was not what I expected.

He casually walked over to me and told me to hold my hand out straight. Then he gave me the biggest four wallops across the palms of my hands that I had ever got. The stick wrapped itself around the backs of my hands. The pain was unbearable. Even now, many, many years on, I can remember the sting. To this day I have no idea why he slapped me. Perhaps, unknown to me, my mother had complained about the time he had made my hand bleed. He had asked me to keep my mouth shut then, but I had gone home and told my mother. Maybe he got in trouble because of this. There was no other reason in my mind for that lashing.

When he was finished he broke the stick in two and threw it in the fire.

* * *

I was not a wimp or a tell-tale, but at times I got tired of Master Dunphy picking on me and I wanted my revenge. There were a few boys that I liked in the school; one was Davey Collins and the other Dick Walshe, Anne's brother. The master was often quite horrible to them as well because they didn't come from "good stock", so to speak. One day, one of them took a razor blade into the school. Before the master got into class, using me as the lookout, the boys sliced the strap that he kept on the table into thin slices. We all sat down in the room awaiting his arrival. We stayed very quiet.

When the master eventually came in he got on with the lessons, not noticing anything unusual. Everything was going fine until someone did something they shouldn't have. They were called to the top of the class for their penance. The master picked up the strap to hit them and it fell to pieces in his hands. The entire class started to laugh and he went berserk. He looked to his spy, the teacher's pet, to tell him who had done it, but his pet didn't have a clue. I had made sure he was not around when it happened. The master was left with no option but to do nothing and I'm sure he felt stupid that day.

On another occasion, Davey and I were in the boy's

playground early one morning and we found some rotten eggs behind one of the big water tanks. We knew we could have a bit of a laugh with our little find. All of a sudden we saw the master himself coming down the road on his bike. We hid behind a big tree and threw the eggs at him full force. They splattered all over his face and clothes, covering him from head to toe. We broke our hearts laughing and ran. He stank the whole day because he couldn't go home to change. Nobody saw us doing it, so nobody could tell, and the master, once again, had no idea who it was.

* * *

The kids from the wealthy families could get away with anything. Because they were teacher's pets they had a free hand to do whatever they wanted, both in the classroom and outside in the playground. I was often picked on by these children, sometimes in the playground, but more often on my way home from school. The name-calling was terrible. One day, some time after I had asked mother the meaning of the word "bastard", I looked it up in a dictionary, and there it was: *bastard – a child born out of wedlock*. I had no idea what wedlock meant and stupidly didn't think of looking it up even though I had the dictionary in my hand. So, I decided to ask my mother again. You would think that I'd have learned my lesson the first time. Her answer was another slap across the face, and a wallop on the legs for good measure. So I decided not to ask again.

There was a boy in school called Eamonn who got away with blue murder. His family were very well known in the village; in fact his father was probably one of the biggest farmers in the county. It goes without saying that Eamonn was one of the untouchables when it came to school. If you so much as put a little finger on little innocent Eamonn his parents would be down to the school the very next morning and you would pay the price.

One day, on my way home from school, he attacked me and beat me with nettles across my legs, calling me all the names he could think of. The final humiliation came when he threw me into a ditch full of mud and briars. I was covered in mud, cut from the briars, and stung with the nettles, and there wasn't anything I could do about it. Or so he thought.

The next evening on the way home Eamonn started the same verbal abuse all over again, only this time he was a little louder, as some of his cronies were with him. I suppose he was trying to show off in front of the lads, making himself out to be the big man. So he started with the usual chant of "Rossie is a bastard, Rossie is a bastard, she has no mother." I had no idea what the hell he was on about; of course I had a mother, didn't I?

I told him to shut up and that he was a snotty-nosed mammy's boy. Without even thinking about it I grabbed him from behind and threw him into the ditch. Then I beat him with a thorny stick and I ran all the way home. He was sick, because his friends were all standing around taking it all in, watching him being beaten up by a girl. I enjoyed every minute of that beating, letting all of my frustration out on this little brat.

But I was to pay the price the next day, as I'd expected.

When I went into school I was pulled to the top of the class and got not four but six slaps of the stick from the master. And when I got home that evening from school I got the mother of all beatings because the teacher must have contacted mother and father to let them know what I had done. Either that or Eamonn's mother had come to the house with all guns blazing.

But I wasn't going to let them all get the better of me. I was used to beatings and I think my body would have been shocked if it hadn't received at least one a week. I decided that this little brat would have to pay for me getting such a hiding. The following evening coming from school I met my tormenter and I did exactly the same thing to him again. I told him that if he went home and told anyone I would beat him even more the next evening. I had gone past caring about the consequences, and decided that no matter what they did to me I wasn't going to be pushed around any longer by this snotty-nosed twerp. Needless to say, his teasing stopped. It was great for once to feel that someone was scared of me, because it was usually the other way round.

* * *

It was in school that I first got a hint that I wasn't who my family said I was. Sometimes in class the master would call me Áine. He did it so often that I began automatically to answer to it. I decided one day to get to the heart of the matter.

"Master, why do you call me Áine?"

"Because that's your real name."

I was surprised and said, "My real name is Rossie, not Áine."

His reply was casual and offhand. "You only answer to that because that's what the Nolans call you." What he said next really shocked me. "You're not even a Nolan."

Stunned, I asked him, "If I'm not a Nolan, then who am I?"

But he refused to be drawn any further. "You'll just have to ask the Nolans that."

That evening, as if I hadn't learned my lesson before, I asked my mother, "Is my name Rossie or Áine?"

I knew instantly that something was wrong. She stared at me and said, "What did you say?"

So I asked again.

I never saw the hand coming but I sure enough felt it land on the side of my face.

"Who have you been talking to? Who put that rubbish into your head?"

I wondered if I should tell her what the master said in case it came back on me; but I knew she wouldn't let it go so I decided to spill the beans.

"Master Dunphy calls me Áine and I asked him why as my name is Rossie. He told me it isn't Rossie, it's Áine." I paused, took a deep breath and said, "He also told me that I'm not a Nolan, but he wouldn't tell me who I am. He just said I should ask you." I was on a roll, so I continued: "The other children call me a bastard all the time."

Cool as you like, she replied, "That's because you are."

One of the kids had filled me in on what "wedlock" meant, so I shot back at her, "Well you and father can't be married then, because a bastard is a baby whose mother and father are not married."

This time I saw the sweeping brush coming and I made a run for it.

The next day, the master was called out to the school door on "private business". As we were a nosy lot, someone looked out to see who it was and shouted, "Rossie, it's your mother." I thought, *Oh no, I'm in big trouble now*. But he never said a word when he came back to the classroom and I never did find out any more. It didn't take much to figure out that his cards had been marked for him. I felt a bit sorry for him that day.

* * *

Every summer I was sent away to a nearby town to stay with my foster mother's cousins. They had three children; the eldest was William, who was two years younger than I was. I recall a time when I was crying and wanted to go home, as I did not like William's mother – she always made me scrub the floors and polish everything. Her husband Jim was a vet and he took William and me off to Dublin for the day to cheer me up. When we were coming back to his house he asked me, "You don't really want to go home now, do you?" Of course I said no because I had enjoyed my day with him, so he let me stay for the whole summer until the beginning of September when the school term started. He obviously knew what was happening in our house and in his own way he probably felt he was helping me without getting too involved.

On other occasions Jim would bring William and me out with him on calls to the farms, which I really loved, as he was the kindest person I knew at that time. When he was finished his rounds with the farmers he would stop off at a pub to have a drink. He always bought us a glass of lemonade. It was a real treat for me.

One particular day when he did this, William and I stayed outside in the sand pit playing. I was about twelve at the time. A car drove up and four men got out of it. They stood looking at William and me for a minute, and then one of them came over and spoke to me.

"You're Áine, aren't you, and you live in Clara?"

I was a bit taken aback and said, "No, my name is Rossie."

"It is not Rossie – who told you it was Rossie?"

"That's what everyone calls me."

He put his hands on my shoulders and said, "Your name is Áine and it is really lovely to see you." He gently touched my face with his hand and walked off into the pub.

I wondered for a brief moment how he knew what he claimed to know. But as a child you don't tend to think too much about things; you just accept what adults say and don't question it too much.

William and I continued playing for a few minutes and then we went into the bar to get a glass of Coke. I noticed the four men sitting down at a table having a drink. I asked Jim if he knew who they were and he said that they were the Gardaí. Jim asked why I wanted to know, and I told him that one of them knew me; he knew who I was and where I lived and told me that my name was not Rossie but Áine.

I have never seen anyone jump off a seat as quickly as I

saw Jim do that day. He grabbed me by the hand and called to William and we left the pub in such a hurry that he never finished his drink.

Needless to say, Jim never took me back to that pub after that day. I always wondered who the men were and how they knew me and, of course, why they thought my name was Áine, the same name my teacher in school had sometimes used. Nobody ever mentioned that day to me or questioned me about what was said and it was only years later that I realised how odd it was.

* * *

Every summer when I came back home I would go down to the bottom of the field behind our house to have a chat with a man called Jack who lived in a little house there. He was a lovely man and I went to school with his sons. Jack's wife died when his children were very young but he did everything he could to look after the kids on his own.

I got on great with him and I would drop down to fill him in on my summer and catch up on everything that had happened while I was away. I told him that I never knew why mother always sent me away and I remember Jack saying one day, "Well, I know why. The reason she sends you away is because your people come during the summer to try to see you and she doesn't want you here when that happens."

Of course I didn't know what he was talking about at the time and when I asked him who he meant by "your people", he just shrugged his shoulders. I know now that he was too scared to cross the boundary and tell me the truth and he probably thought I was too young to understand anyway. If my foster parents had known that I was speaking to Jack I would have been in deep trouble, as I was not allowed to talk to anyone when I was living there. I never saw anyone to speak to anyway, so I used to tell Jack not to say that I called down to him and he always kept his word. He knew in his heart what would happen if they ever found out.

But I always enjoyed our little chats.

* * *

Despite the obstacles, I enjoyed school because it meant getting out of that house. I was keen on learning everything and did quite well in most subjects, apart from algebra, which I just could not get to grips with, no matter how hard I tried.

I recall one lesson in particular. The master must have told me the solution three times but I still couldn't get it. Finally he asked me if I was deaf. Quick as a flash, I told him I was. I only said it so that he would leave me alone. It seemed to work because he looked quite shocked, so I thought nothing more of it. However, when it came to break time, he called me back and asked me if I really was deaf. I had put my foot in it already and there was no going back now, so I said I was, in my right ear. He told me that it was okay and to go back out to play. With that I skipped off happily to the playground, grinning to myself and thinking that I had got away with it. He was quite easy on me for the rest of the day, which made me very happy.

Alas, my happiness was short-lived. That evening as I was working at home, I noticed from the corner of my eye that the master was standing at the gate talking to my mother. I wondered what they were talking about and I racked my brains, trying to remember if I had got into trouble either in school or on the way home. I didn't have long to think about it though, for as soon as he had gone I heard my mother shouting to me, "Get in here right now."

She screamed, "What have you been saying in school about you being deaf?"

I groaned.

"I'll give you deaf, you little bitch."

An hour later I was still trying to get the ringing out of my ears from the wallop she planted on the side of my little face.

* * *

I didn't finish sixth class in the national school; I left when I was thirteen and went to the vocational school, which was situated right next door to the house where I lived. I used to climb over the fence to get to it. Being so close to the school was good in one way but bad in another. I could leave the house just five minutes before school started. On the other hand, I couldn't take a "sick day" because there was every chance that I'd be seen by someone from the school if I was out in the back yard or standing at the front door. It was a bit too close for comfort.

However, I did quite well in the vocational school. There were only ten girls in the class. Our teacher was Miss Lynch, who loved to hit her students between the shoulder blades with her fist. The other kids found it hard but it was no big deal for me; I was well used to getting whacked for some reason or none. I just got on with it and knuckled down and eventually I passed all my exams with Honours – including winning a scholarship to train as a chef.

Despite all my hard work and effort my mother could not accept that I had done so well. When I won the scholarship she went up to the school and told Miss Lynch I would not be taking it. She didn't want me to have it because it would have shown up her two daughters (who had failed all their exams) and she could never have accepted that. She told the teacher that she was to give the scholarship to someone else. Miss Lynch put up a fight for me, because she knew how hard I had worked to get the scholarship, but my mother's tongue was too much for her. She eventually relented and gave it to someone else.

To this day this is something that I can never forgive mother for. To make matters worse, when I got my certificates from my exams, she just took them from me and threw them into the fire. "They will never be of any use to you," she said. "No one is going to employ a person like you. Sure, all you'd be good for is scrubbing floors."

I left the vocational school when I was sixteen and that, as far as my mother was concerned, was the end of my education.

CHAPTER FIVE

Glimmers of a New Life

My early teenage years had been a hard slog for me. Not only was I going to school every weekday but I also worked for the local shopkeeper on my time off and I cleaned the vocational school every evening, as well as going into the school early every morning to light the classroom fires. Of course, all of this was on top of the other work I still had to do in the house. I don't remember ever getting a penny for myself for all the work I did back then.

I also worked for a farming family in the locality. The farmer tried to sexually abuse me and I believe would have raped me if he'd had the chance. He used to follow me out into the barns when I had to collect eggs or feed the hens and expose himself to me. He would come up behind me and, with a sly evil grin, licking his ugly fat lips, pull down his zip and take his penis out. He would walk towards me with it in his hands and I would run away, disgusted. It happened quite a lot, so I spent much of my time there trying to keep out of his way. Whenever he came into the house he would give me such a leering look that I would either walk straight out or go upstairs. I have no idea if his wife knew what was going on. They had so many children they were like steps of stairs and she didn't have a minute to herself.

Such things used to happen to me on regular occasions when I was sent to "help out" on these farms, as the adults called it. I now feel that this kind of abuse occurred because of *what* I was, not *who* I was. Everyone knew I was a "bastard", so I was no good and never would be, as I was told so many times during my childhood and teenage years. I think some men saw this as an excuse or a reason to try to force themselves on me. They saw me as a bastard, a child resulting from dirty sex between a woman who wasn't married and a man, married or not. I was just a piece of dirt in their eyes and there to be abused. I think that when people put you down so often you tend to accept it and even, I suppose, believe it. I chose then to believe that this abuse happened because of what I was. I never told anybody at home about it in case they told me exactly the same thing. I could cope with saying it to myself but not when they told me.

* * *

When I left school at sixteen I got a job as a nanny-cum-housekeeper. I don't remember applying for the job, nor did

I go for an interview and I don't even remember being given a choice as to whether I wanted the job or not. I was simply told that I was going to work for this family and that was that.

The Black family – Dr and Mrs Black and their three young children – lived not too far away from our home, in a village I shall call Stoney. I wasn't allowed to call the parents by their first names so it was always "Dr" and "Mrs" to me. They lived in a big house just outside the little village. I was given my own room in their home, which was really nice, as the window looked out into the woods to the rear. It was very compact. It had just the basics of a single bed, a wardrobe and a chest of drawers, but it was ample space for the very few clothes that I had. I hung my Sunday best coat proudly in the wardrobe. At first it felt very strange waking up in the morning and not being at home. I had no fire to light or sticks to bring in, no hens or pigs to feed and clean out, and most of all no bellowing from my mother. It felt like heaven.

I was told what my duties were: to do all the housework, which included cleaning, washing, ironing, sewing and looking after the three children, who were all under five. I was to have my meals in the kitchen either with the children or on my own when the children were in bed. I had to make sure that the dining room table was laid for their meals each day. This suited me just fine. I was well used to eating on my own anyway. I was just happy to be away from home and I felt all grown up at the ripe old age of sixteen.

The man of the house, Dr Black, was the local GP. I have no idea what Mrs Black did, but she didn't help me out. She was in the house most of the time but she chose to stay in her room on her own and allowed me to care for her children without any interference.

I stayed with the family for about three months, then one day they told me they had made a decision to move to England. Dr Black was going to train as a surgeon, so he was moving all the family over to a town in Essex. They asked my mother if I could go with them and, to my surprise, she said yes. I have no idea if there were any conditions laid down as I was still under twenty-one and under the care of my foster parents.

In order to travel to the UK, I needed my birth certificate. There was a commotion in the house over whether it should be given to me, but in the end mother relented.

I will never forget the day. Without flinching, without looking embarrassed and without an explanation, she handed me my birth certificate, saying, "This is what you will need. And I wouldn't take much heed of what's written on it." I didn't know what she was on about and asked her what she meant, but she wouldn't say anymore.

When I looked at the sheet of official paper I couldn't believe what I was reading. It said that my name was Anastasia O'Brien, not Rossie Nolan, and that I was born on the 10th of August 1950. In my sixteen years it was the first time I knew my name and date of birth and it felt very odd. It felt very peculiar knowing that the name I had been called for all those years was false. My whole life to that very day had been a lie.

Seeing my birth date in black-and-white in front of me was weird. I still find it hard to believe that through all my life with this family they had never told me my date of birth. I could understand in a way why they wanted to keep my name a secret from me, so as not to have me asking questions, but they could have gone along with the birth date and got away with it. I had once asked why I never had a birthday party every year like Kate and Nancy and the other children in school. I was told that nobody wanted to know the day I was born as "bastards don't have birthdays". It was a day that no one cared to remember and everyone would like to forget. I was always hurt by this and always longed for a birthday party like everyone else but of course it never came. I had to be content enjoying myself as much as I could at my sisters' fancy parties, which of course I cooked and cleaned for.

Now I had seen the birth certificate, what I had suspected was confirmed: I wasn't their daughter. Nobody asked me if I was all right after learning this shocking piece of news, this bolt from the blue. They never sat me down to explain how I came to be living with them, why they took me in or why they had never told me before that I wasn't actually their child.

Suddenly all the bad things that had happened to me were explained. It all fell into place, without a word being said. They had hated me because I wasn't theirs to love in the first place. Could that have been the reason all along for all the hatred, bitterness and beatings? However, I quickly realised that all the answers I wanted definitely weren't going to come that day. I left that afternoon with my head filled with hundreds of unanswered questions but with a heart filled with relief and hope.

* * *

Getting my birth certificate was like finding a piece of treasure, or a key that would open some great doors of opportunity for me, doors that had been locked for so long. Now that I knew I was not a Nolan I could start searching for my real family, my other life and hopefully a better future. Holding that piece of paper in my hand made me realise that I had actually never felt like a Nolan. Seeing my real name written down made me happier than I had ever been in my whole short, manic life.

I thought of the master in school and how he had known all along that I wasn't a Nolan. I was grateful to him for preparing me somewhat for this shock.

Despite all the excitement of finally being given an identity, after all those years of slavery, I knew that I had no time now to start questioning and searching, as I had to move to Essex to start my new life. Little did the Black family realise, when they asked me to go with them, that instead of just giving me a job they were also giving me a life, one I had never had or could never have dreamt of before.

I prepared for my trip and bid my very brief and unemotional goodbyes to my family, the Nolans, and headed off with the Blacks. There were no tears, no long goodbyes; I was just moving on. We took the boat from Dublin to Holyhead, then the train to Euston station in London. This was the first time I had been on any form of transport other than a car or a bus. We settled into a house in the grounds of a big hospital where Dr Black was to do his training. It took a few weeks for us all to get sorted but things seemed to be going fine.

Despite being given my new identity and being set free, I still had to send most of what I earned home to Ireland as my mother would write every week telling me that I owed them a fortune for all the costs involved in raising me. I often wondered what money they had actually spent, as I lived in hand-me-downs and I mostly ate bread and margarine. So how they could say that I owed them a fortune was beyond me. But to save any trouble I sent the money home. I wasn't going out socialising anyway so I wasn't spending very much. If it kept them satisfied and out of my life then I was only too happy to oblige.

After about six months I started to notice changes in Mrs Black. Both she and Dr Black were constantly arguing and he came down to breakfast some mornings with scratches on his face. I had no idea what was going on, nor did I want to know as the children were my concern; Mrs Black was hardly spending any time with them, not even to take the eldest to playschool. The atmosphere in the house was not good; Mrs Black began picking on everything I did or didn't do. At sixteen I found all this rather hard. I spoke to the doctor and he said that they were going through a bit of a tough time and that things would get better. Things did settle down after a while and we were all getting on fine. I think she may have started taking anti-depressants to get her through the days.

* * *

One night after I had got the children to bed and I was cleaning up in the kitchen, a knock came at the door. The doctor answered it and there stood two policemen with my foster sister Nancy. I was called to the front room and I nearly died when I saw my sister standing there. My mind was racing, trying to figure out what I had done wrong for her to be here, especially with the police. She had a face like thunder. I couldn't think of a thing that could have been wrong but knew I must have done something really bad that I had been totally unaware of and I got very scared.

One of the policemen must have guessed how I was feeling by the look on my face. He stepped forward and said that they had been sent by my foster mother and that I was to go back to Ireland as I was still under their care. I couldn't understand why she had suddenly changed her mind after so long. I tried to explain to the officers that everything was fine and that mother had agreed to me going away with the Blacks, but he told me that I didn't have a choice in the matter. Nancy would take me to the airport in the morning; I was to leave with her that night and stay in her place until the next day. I looked at Nancy pleadingly for any signs of why this was happening but all I saw in her face was contempt.

I packed up my few belongings and I left the Blacks that night, absolutely heartbroken. I could not believe that I was going back to Ireland, to a life I had been sure was well and truly behind me. Dr and Mrs Black were shocked by the whole thing but even they could do nothing. The police took me out to a car and we drove to Nancy's flat some miles away. I knew she lived nearby, but she had never contacted me in all my time there and no one had given me an address. I still don't know where I was taken that day as Nancy's husband was driving and nothing much was said in the car. Now I was never fond of Nancy and at times she scared me; she could be very much like her mother, nasty and aggressive. Her tongue would cut you in two. Despite all this, during the drive I decided to confront her.

"Nancy, why do I have to go home? Why has mother changed her mind all of a sudden? I've done nothing wrong!"

Nancy turned around in her seat and said, "You've done nothing wrong? Well, think again, miss. Did you honestly think that my mother would let you get away with it?"

"I don't know what you're talking about." I was genuinely mystified.

"Yes you do. Look, we'll sort it out when we get to the flat – until then, you can think long and hard about what you've done wrong."

So I sat in the back of the car, wrecking my head trying to think what the hell I could have done wrong. From the way that Nancy was carrying on I felt that I must have done something horrific. It brought back memories of what my life had been like; my first thought on waking every morning was, *Did I do anything wrong last night that would get me a beating this morning?* Here I was again, going through the same fear. And then it suddenly dawned on me.

During the time that the Blacks had been having problems, I had taken on full care of the children, morning, noon and night, without taking time off. They had been getting quite stressed and, as I love children, I could not bear to see them being upset. I didn't have the time to do anything for myself. So during this time I forgot to send money home to mother and I hadn't answered any of her letters. I wondered now if she was getting her revenge.

When we arrived at the flat, I asked Nancy if it was because I hadn't sent money home. She snapped back, "Yes, and I will have any money you have on you now and make sure my mother gets it." I couldn't believe that this was happening simply because this woman, who wasn't even my mother, and who had abused me from the very day she took me under her roof, had not received a few weeks' wages.

I asked Nancy, "Do you send money home?"

Of course, this didn't go down well. "It's none of your business what I do."

As far as I was concerned, this meant that she didn't. My foster mother's own flesh and blood got away with sending nothing home whilst I had to continue supporting her family, when I wasn't even living there.

Without another word she told me to show her all of the money I had on me and she took nearly everything. She left me with just ten shillings and told me that I would be flying home the next day and I wasn't to spend any of this money on trash. I was to spend the tiny amount she had given me on my bus fare from Dublin to my home county and nothing else.

The next morning I was dumped off at a busy airport where I boarded a plane for Ireland. I had never flown before and I was totally terrified. My stomach was in a knot and I wanted to get off the flight as soon as I could. I was scared stiff taking off and I felt every little bump all the way home. At one stage I was bursting to go to the toilet but I was so naive that I almost believed that if I stood up to walk the plane would topple sideways and we would all die. So I sat petrified and stuck to the seat for the whole flight home. I can't remember how I got from Dublin back home, but I managed somehow.

When I eventually got to the house, some hours later, there was no welcome home. Mother never spoke a word to me, ignoring me as if I wasn't even there. She didn't even give out to me for not sending the money or say why she had sent the police to get me to come back. Nothing. Every time I tried to speak to her she would just say that there was nothing that I could say that would be of interest to her. I remember thinking, *Then why the hell did you want me to come home at all? Could I not just have sent the bloody money and stayed where I was?*

About a week after I got back, having been ignored for the whole time by everyone, I decided that I would try to get talking to them – even if they wanted nothing to do with me. I hadn't mixed with them at all since coming home. I took my food each day when they weren't around and sat in my room alone. But this time I went to sit down at the table. My mother said, "What the hell are you doing?"

"I'm hungry," I said, "and I'm going to sit down with you."

She jumped out of her chair. "Who told you that you can eat? You no longer eat in this house when you are not working and giving me money. Do I make myself clear?"

I was angry. I got up immediately and headed out the door. I went straight to my friend Tricia's house where I got very upset and told her mother Bridie everything. She was gobsmacked, but spoke kindly to me. "Don't you worry about anything. What we have in this house is yours." I knew they had little enough for themselves, and her generosity touched me deeply.

Tricia had such a different upbringing to me, one I now know to be normal. But at the time I thought she was really special to have such a caring mother. Bridie was like the mother I never had but always craved. She loved her daughter so much and even though they had very little money Tricia was always fed well and told by her mam how much she was loved.

It was to Tricia's house that I would run whenever I could escape. She wasn't allowed into my home – no one was allowed visit me – but Tricia's front door was always open to everyone. When I would arrive up at the house Bridie would jump up and start cooking for me. She obviously knew the circumstances at the Nolans and I'd say Tricia told her how badly treated I was. So she was like a mother hen when I would arrive and she could never do enough for me. She always told me that I was welcome any time to their home and I was never to go hungry. She was a lady. I loved going up there because I always came home happy, having been fed and chatted to for ages.

They had the home I always dreamt of. Tricia had toys, dolls and a bike and she always loved me to come over so we could play together. It was like another world to me. The house was only about ten minutes' walk away from mine so I could run up and back fairly quickly and most times no one even noticed that I was gone. Tricia had nice clothes too, not like mine. They weren't expensive but they were hers.

Tricia and her mam were lifesavers for me.

* * *

It wasn't long before I struck lucky and got a job in a town nearby with an older couple who had no children. They were good people, but the wife used to drink quite a lot of gin and orange. In fact she drank so much that I would find the sticky glasses all over the house, as she used to hide them from her husband. He would follow her around the place like a lap dog, probably trying to stop her drinking. My job there was to cook and clean and make sure that they had everything they needed. They looked after me very well and I was always grateful to them for taking me away from my family and giving me a chance to gain at least a bit of independence. Of course, my wages were sent home to my mother every week and I hardly saw any of it, but I didn't care because I was my own person.

The job also meant that I slept in with the family. I had a room on the opposite side of the main house. The bedroom was quite creepy, though, because it was so far away from where the couple slept and I was all alone. The only thing I had for company were the rats. There was many a night when I lay awake for hours listening to their claws scraping away on the floorboards. I was too terrified to sleep. For the most part, though, I enjoyed my time there and I was sad when they sold their house and moved into a smaller house more suitable for just the two of them. Once they moved they didn't need me anymore and once again I was unemployed.

Before I finished up with them, however, they got me a job in Dublin. I moved up there without any argument from the Nolans. This new family lived in the leafy suburb of Foxrock on the outskirts of Dublin. They were a very wealthy family; he had a very important job in the government – so important that when I got the job they sent a car to collect me from my home to take me to my new position. No train or buses for me this time. I felt like a lady being chauffeured all the way to the capital with my own driver. I enjoyed working with them and they were a lovely family.

Unfortunately, after trouble broke out in Northern Ireland, things got very tough for them. The man of the house had a big part to play in trying to maintain calm during the Troubles and it had a devastating effect on his life and his family. I used to pick up the phone to hear threatening voices telling me that they knew who I was and who my friends were. They didn't, of course, but they were just trying to freak out the family. I was still very young and I didn't grasp the seriousness of all the threats. The calls were a regular occurrence and on one occasion when this happened I lost my cool and told them to "piss off". For a while I thought that it was someone playing a joke. It wasn't until I told one of the Special Branch officers who patrolled the house about what was happening and I casually explained to them about the phone calls that I realised that things must have been bad.

The seriousness of it all finally came home to me when I was coming back after a night out with two of my friends. I was walking up the drive when I thought I saw someone in the bushes. My heart started to race but I pretended not to notice. Then I saw someone walking behind me so I ran to the house and banged the door down in a panic. Dave the security guard opened it and I ran straight past him. He was shouting, "What's the matter, did something happen to you?"

When I eventually got my breath back I said to him, "You'll never guess what I saw!"

"What, what?"

"There are some men roaming around the garden."

"Oh God, Ann – we forgot to tell you that there are security men all around the house and the family will be moving to Cork tomorrow. We will get you to the train station tomorrow after the family leaves."

I couldn't believe it. I loved my job and now a problem in Northern Ireland, miles away from Dublin, meant that I couldn't work for this family, whom I really liked, anymore. I hadn't realised until that moment just how dangerous it was being in their home, and now it was all over. The family left early the next morning and I was very upset. The press called to the front door later in the day. I was about to open it when Dave came rushing down the hallway and said that I was not to tell them anything – not that I knew what "anything" might be.

On the front page of the evening paper later I read in an article that "a pale-faced country girl" had opened the door to the reporter. Me, a pale-faced girl!

I left Dublin that evening and went back home to stay with my friend Tricia until I got another job. Mother and father didn't argue as they knew that I was looking for work and their money would start coming in again. And as long as I was with Tricia it didn't cost them anything to look after me, so they were fine with it.

A few weeks after I moved back, I got another job as a nanny and housekeeper with a family called the Kellys. The father was the editor of a local newspaper in another county and they were absolutely lovely. I lived-in with this family as well and things worked out fine. I continued to send money home and everyone was happy.

I stayed with the Kellys until just before my twenty-first birthday. Then, I thought, the world would become my oyster.

CHAPTER SIX

Coming of Age

As I approached my twenty-first birthday, I began to think about getting away, and Tricia and I began to make plans. She had been my lifeline throughout my teenage years. We both wanted bigger and better things and the only way to get a better life was to move away from our little village to a big city with lots of jobs and better pay. And that's why we chose London. This trip would be like a dream come true for both of us.

We decided that I would be the one to make all the plans; Tricia said she would just go along with whatever I organised. I started reading the job pages in the *Irish Independent* and noticed that there were quite a few positions up for grabs in the big city. I contacted an agency in Dublin called Brophy's and told them I was interested in work for myself and my friend in London. They asked me to come and meet them, so on my next day off (I was still working for the Kellys) I headed to Dublin for an interview. The interviewer asked me about myself and Tricia and then told me that there was a job going in a nursing home in London which might suit us. They needed two people in about six or eight weeks' time. It sounded perfect and I agreed that we would be delighted to take the jobs.

They told me that the couple who ran the place were Irish, which immediately relaxed me. I felt it was a case of "better the devil you know". The timing was spot on – just after my birthday, so mother couldn't stop me from going. Of course the only reason she didn't want me to go anywhere was because she would be losing out on her extra money for my keep.

I couldn't wait to tell Tricia the good news. When she heard it she was as excited as me about the prospect of a new life outside the confines of our little village where if you sneezed somebody two miles away would hear you had a cold. The idea of total freedom was so exciting for both of us. I couldn't wait to stand on my own two feet finally. I had built up a good circle of friends when I worked in the town but most of them never knew about my life at home, as I chose not to tell them, so it wouldn't be too difficult for me to make the break from them. My closest friend has and always will be Tricia and once I had her by my side I knew that I'd be fine. Tricia's mam wasn't married either and just like me Tricia had to grow up with the stigma of being illegitimate.

The only thing that bothered me was that I was already working and living with a lovely family in the town and I had a few doubts about whether or not I was doing the right thing. But I knew in my heart that I had to get away from Ireland. I really wanted to get away from the life that I was leading, pretending that things were okay when they clearly weren't. I was sick and tired of hearing what people thought of me. I just wanted to go where no one knew who I was.

Also, I didn't want to get pregnant like some of the local girls I knew, who had ended up marrying older men simply to keep their parents happy. Thankfully the one thing that I had kept throughout my life was my self-respect.

So despite all the worries and hesitations, Tricia and I were going to be heading off into the sunset, to a new life in a country where no one knew anything about us. We were wound up with excitement.

* * *

I never had a birthday like other children, as I didn't know my date of birth until I got my birth certificate at the age of sixteen. I never had a party, never a day that was "my special day" with the family; in fact, I never even got a present. So I was determined that my twenty-first was going to be different. Most people associate their twenty-first with getting the key of the door, but for me it was a key to unlock the chains that had kept me in that house of painful memories and a ruined childhood, where my innocence was robbed from me so callously.

So was I going to celebrate my big day? Try stopping me! The date was the 10th of August 1971. How I waited for this date to come around! It was my coming-of-age birthday and no one was going to stop me from having a party, albeit in my house with no friends. I had earlier asked my mother when I got her on a good day if I could have a tea party at the house for my twenty-first and she had surprisingly said yes. I asked if Kate and her husband could come and she said that she would ask them. There would have been no point in sending out any other invitations as I knew that nobody would be welcome. It wasn't that I didn't have friends – I did – but I had planned to celebrate with them when I went back to town. I had planned this house party with the family for months. My mother would certainly not have allowed me to bring my friends into the house. The other girls were allowed to have their pals in whenever they wanted. However, it didn't bother me in the least because, come hell or high water, I, Anastasia O'Brien, was having a party.

However, to ensure that everything ran like clockwork, I had to make certain that I gave my foster mother more than enough money to keep her happy. If I hadn't lined her pockets well that week she would probably have pulled the plug on the whole celebration without another thought, so I had made sure that she was more than happy with my donation to the day. I was going to buy myself a birthday cake and put twenty-one candles on it. I planned to make some little cakes and an assortment of sandwiches and buy some drinks, maybe even some beers. Not that I actually would have drunk any of the beer myself – that was a definite no-no! No one in that house knew that I took a drink every now and then. They didn't know that I drank when I was out with my friends. But I had decided myself anyway that on this day I would forgo my favourite drink, a little bottle of Babycham. Instead, I would toast my birthday with a glass of ginger beer and buy in some beers for the rest of them. I had decided that they would all be there this day to toast my freedom. But of course they didn't know that. They didn't realise that the birthday gathering was all part of my plan to tell them of my intention of heading off to England.

I was surprised that my foster sister and her husband actually turned up, but they did. They all did (except my other sister Nancy, who was still in England working at the time). So I sat there on the day with these people whom I knew despised me – and I smiled like I had never smiled before. For that day, at least, I was the happiest person in Ireland. I didn't really want to be surrounded by those people on that day; at one stage I looked around and asked myself, *What am I doing with these people here?* In my heart of hearts I knew what I was doing, and I also knew that I was deliberately pushing the boundaries a little in my favour. This is why I softened my mother with the money beforehand; I didn't want to give her any further excuses to turn on me. I also knew that I was treading on new territory and had to be careful, especially if I was going to announce my departure for England. Yet I was still torturing myself by being around them, especially on a day like this, a day that everyone remembers for the rest of their lives. Most people have surprise parties thrown by their parents for all their friends and relatives; others go away on a big holiday with their pals; and everyone gets special presents from their families. All I got was a big fat nothing. But I didn't really expect anything, not even a card – never did, never have, and

ANN KENNY

never will. I didn't let it bother me. What they didn't realise was that I had been hatching this plan in my head for months, and I wanted them all there to hear what I needed to say.

They knew that I wasn't myself that day; I was much too happy, not the usual Rossie at all. I could see them all waiting for whatever was coming, hanging onto my every word. So, when they were all sitting down, tucking into the goodies I had prepared, I raised my glass. As I looked up I made a silent wish and a promise to myself that life was going to get better. Then I said out loud, "Happy Birthday, Rossie." As I said it, I thought to myself, *That name has to go now*. I had it long enough and it did not belong in my new life.

I didn't get much of a response, just a grunt from mother and father. I don't think my sister even flinched. She kept her head down as I raised my glass. There would have been more atmosphere in a morgue than there was around that table.

However, as I looked around at their faces I decided that I wouldn't tell them about my plans just yet. They knew that I was dying to tell them something, as I was far too chatty, not my usual self at all. But something held me back from telling them – fear, I suppose. And as there were four of them there I don't think I would have been able to cope with the backlash. It would be much easier, I decided, breaking the news to my foster parents on their own and I realised there and then that even the best laid plans sometimes don't necessarily work. So I decided, just for the moment anyway, to hold my tongue. I would let myself enjoy this day as it was, the first and last birthday party I would ever have in this house. I decided that I would break the good news to mother in a few days' time, leaving them to wonder what exactly I had up my sleeve.

Telling them about my new life would just have to wait a little longer.

* * *

It would be another two weeks after my birthday before I broke the news to my foster family. I left the house that day and went back to work in the town with the Kelly family.

Returning two weeks later, I called up to the house and father had told me that mother had gone to see one of the neighbours. I stood looking at my father for a minute, wondering if I should tell him my plans before I broke the news to her. He was an odd man who showed little or no emotion and as I looked at him that day I felt a sorrow for him. I realised that for all those years he had been beaten down by my mother, made into a little lapdog to obey her every command. He wasn't really a man at all; he too was one of her servants. As I looked at his ageing face, wrinkled brow, stooped frame and greying hair, I decided to tell him first.

"I just wanted to let you know that I'm going away for good and making a new life for myself."

He asked me where I was going and I told him I was heading off to England. I deliberately didn't tell him that I was going to London.

He looked up at me from his armchair, stood up and simply said, "I knew you would go as soon as you turned twenty-one, when there was nothing anyone could do to stop you, and I really don't blame you." This took me by surprise as my father never showed the slightest bit of interest in what I did as long as I was giving them money. He went on, "Sure, it may be the best thing that you do. You were always strong and stubborn, no matter what she did to you."

Those words hurt me instead of comforting me, because I now realised for sure that he knew exactly how she had treated me and had never done a thing to stop it. He had seen me beaten, tortured and dozens of other unspeakable things happen to me and he had just sat back and let her carry on. Throughout the years I had always imagined that he didn't really know what was happening. If he did, surely he would have stepped in and stopped it?

I tried to hold back my tears. I didn't tell him how I felt. I just said goodbye and told him that I would see mother over the road.

He simply shook my hand and said, "She is not going to like it, but you know that already, don't you?"

"I do, but this time she can't stop me because I'm old enough to do what I want and she has no hold over me."

As I walked away I felt no regret, no sorrow and no love.

I eventually caught up with my mother as I cycled along the road. She was a bit surprised to see me. I got off the bike and walked beside her.

"I have something to tell you," I began.

"There is nothing that you have to say that is of any interest to me."

"Well, I'm going to tell you anyway." I took a deep breath and said, "I am going to England."

She stopped in her tracks, turned to me and said, "What? You're going to England? Who said you're going to England?"

"I've made the decision for myself and there's nothing you can do about it now that I'm twenty-one."

She got all steamed up and started to breathe deeply in and out as she walked, shouting, "We'll see about that."

I snapped back, "You can see about it all you like, but the fact is I'm going whether you like it or not. You have no control or power over me to stop it."

She stopped once again, turned and looked at me with such venom in her eyes. "Remember, miss, I put a stop to you before and I'll do it again."

I couldn't believe her reaction. If she hated me so much, why was she annoyed that I was finally leaving her life for good? Calmly and quietly, I told her, "I'm well aware of how you wrecked my chance in England the last time. But this time I'm an adult, not under your care, and I will do as I please from now on."

I could see that she was really irritated by this. She swung around and shouted, "Because you're twenty-one you think you're so smart, don't you, coming here to tell me that you're going to England. You won't last two weeks there, miss, and see how smart you will be then!" She said no more, just turned her back on me and stomped off up the road.

I stood at the side of that old country road, shaking. My insides were like jelly. I knew what it took for me to face her. I was surprised that I had stood my ground and not backed down when she had become aggressive and domineering. I was glad that I had done it.

I turned my bike around, jumped on the saddle and cycled back to the city. I tried to concentrate on the road and not on what had happened, but I was still shaking inside. By the time I got there I had calmed down. But I did wonder if I would ever see either of them again, or if I would ever want to for that matter. I know it was not the best way to say "goodbye". It was not the way I would have liked to remember our parting; but then again there weren't many memories for me to take from the life I was leaving. I had always made excuses for them throughout my life, sometimes blaming myself for annoying them or doing something when they lashed out at me. The truth was, I was always the innocent party. They had simply used me as a target to take out all of their frustration and anger.

But I told myself that was all in the past now and I had my whole life to look forward to with a new identity in a new country. I was making the move to England with my best pal and hopefully I would never have to come back. It was a bit harder for Tricia to make the break, of course, because she had a great mother and they had a great relationship, so unlike me it was very hard for her to pack up and say her goodbyes.

As far as I was concerned this day was the beginning of the rest of my life.

* * *

I shall never forget the morning when we finally arrived in the big city, where, according to everyone back in Ireland, the streets were said to be paved with gold. We had taken the boat from Dun Laoghaire to Holyhead and we were both excited and terrified. How would we survive in a totally alien country?

I had of course been in England for a while with the Black family but I had been very young and immature back then. In fact, I hadn't realised I was in Essex until about two weeks after I got there! I was the stereotypical country girl.

Tricia and I arrived at the ferry port and took a train into Euston Station in the heart of London, in the middle of rush hour, with all our worldly goods. We were two frightened, tired, innocent young Irish girls. We had jobs, but we had no idea what we were going to do or how things were going to work out for us. We knew that we had to get to Ealing but we had no idea how to get there. Unfortunately there were no computers around back then to make life easy. We eventually asked a man for help and he told us to go down the escalator and get the tube to Ealing Broadway.

This new world of "tubes" and "escalators" was very strange to us. We had never heard any of these words before. But we didn't want to appear too green so we just said thanks to the man and headed off to find a sign that said "escalator". It was such a different set-up to what we were used to in our little hometown. We were typical Irish country girls lost in the big city. There seemed to be thousands of people everywhere, like ants, rushing around the place. Nobody seemed to stop for long.

We had never been on an escalator before and when I saw

the tube my mouth dropped. I couldn't believe how many people crammed onto these things and how quickly they pulled in, filled up and pulled out. For a moment I wanted to be back home where everything was simple, with no moving stairs or trains that ate people up. I was thinking, *What in the name of God am I doing here? If my mother could only see me now she would die laughing at how I'm unable to cope alone in the big bad world*. But that very thought made me even more determined to make this move a success. There was no way I ever wanted to admit defeat to my family. We might be in a strange country but we were going to grab every opportunity by the horns and make the most of every minute of it.

When we finally got to Ealing Broadway, we got into a black taxi and told the driver the address we were looking for. It took us about half an hour to get to the place and the driver charged us nearly £3, which was a lot back then. It was only when we were there a few weeks and got to know the place that we discovered it was only a seven-minute drive from the station to the care home where we were working. It should have cost a little over a pound. That first taxi driver must have seen the green in our eyes and our strong Irish country accents would have given the game away as soon as we opened our mouths.

* * *

The nursing home was two old houses broken into one. We were met by Joan, who was heavily pregnant, and her sister Rose. Joan owned the place and her sister was only there to help her out until we arrived.

It wasn't exactly the perfect welcoming party. Tricia and I were worn out with all the travelling and we were both looking forward to having some sleep and starting work in the morning. However, our plan was shattered very quickly when Joan told us, after a little tour of the place, that we were to start there and then. I think she could see the shock in our faces and she relented a little and showed us to our rooms, telling us that we could have just two hours' rest. Then we would be expected downstairs to get our instructions and to commence work.

Joan, who actually single-handedly ran the home, was Irish herself so I thought she would have been a bit more understanding. When we got upstairs Tricia said to me, "What part of Ireland are these pair from? Do they not know that slavery went out years ago?"

I was in too much shock to respond. I am a terrible person for making judgements about people and I just didn't like Rose at all, from the moment I set eyes on her. I have no idea why, but she seemed to have touched a few buttons of mine. I didn't say any of this to Tricia; I didn't want to worry her any more than she was already.

I didn't sleep a wink. I just lay on the bed, my brain in overdrive, wondering if it would all work out. Had I jumped from the frying pan into the fire in my desperate bid to leave my hometown and escape my family?

When we went downstairs two hours later, we were met by Rose in the kitchen. She told us that Joan was resting and would be down later to have a chat with us and familiarise us with the place. She then told us that she had done out a rota for us and put it in the utility room. We were to look at it and follow what was on it each day.

With that she walked out of the kitchen and left us both standing there like twits. No more direction. She said nothing about the patients living there, what we were to do for them or what special needs some may have had. She didn't even introduce us to any of them or tell us their names. Nothing. Tricia and I looked at each other, wondering what to do next. We headed over to the utility room where we found the rota pinned up on the wall. I stood there looking at it, my mouth wide open. It even told us what time to get up at! I was really furious at this. Telling us what time to get up at? Who the hell did they think they were? What if we took an extra five minutes in bed? What would it matter once we were ready for work on time?

I asked Tricia, "Have you finished reading it?" When she nodded, I reached up and tore it off the wall, ripping it to pieces.

"What are you doing?" asked Tricia, a look of horror on her face. She was terrified that Rose would come back and kill me.

I looked at her and said, "I might have been a slave back home, but I never worked to a rota in my life and I sure as hell am not going to work to one now!"

What I didn't realise was that the lovely Rose had been watching us all the time as we stood in the utility room. She had seen and heard everything.

Later that evening when Joan appeared, I overheard Rose speaking to her in the living room. I heard her saying, "The dark-haired one (meaning Tricia) is okay, but you may have trouble with the other one." And she told Joan what I had done with the rota. I prepared myself for trouble.

However, when we came down the next morning, Rose was gone and we never saw her again. Joan turned out to be alright, although she was going through a bad time as her husband had run off with the girl who had worked there before us. He had left Joan to cope with the home, her pregnancy and their young daughter called Kitty, whom Tricia and I loved from the minute we met her. She was a beautiful little three-year-old and the most lovable little child you could meet.

Joan was very helpful with us and she filled us in on all the patients who lived there. We were told where they came from, their family backgrounds, their ailments and their individual needs.

There were some great characters. There were two sisters called Flo and Alice. Then there was a lovely old woman who we will call Mrs W; she was in love with one of the men there, an old guy called Bill who suffered with Parkinson's disease. We had another poor old woman who used to love throwing the contents of her commode all over the room. It didn't take me long to change that little habit. One day when she was having one of her fits I carried a bucket of water and a sponge into her room and ordered her to clean it up. I told her that if she didn't clean it she would have to live with the smell of it, for however long it took her to cop on. She wasn't too impressed with me and it took over a week, but eventually I got her to stop throwing the commode about. I was delighted that I had persevered, and so was Joan.

Finally there was Dorothy. She was a lovely lady who used to ramble into my room to try on my clothes. I discovered her little secret one day when she came down for breakfast. I had already got her washed and dressed and left her in her room to do her hair while I went down to attend to breakfast. When she eventually came down she had taken off her own clothes and put on two layers of mine.

* * *

It wasn't long before Tricia and I ended up practically running the whole place. Joan struggled to cope with her little girl, her pregnancy and work. She got very depressed and even stopped looking after Kitty, her daughter. So we took care of her full-time and when baby George arrived we did the same for him.

Joan had started to swallow back sleeping tablets as if they were sweets. In the end I had no choice but to phone her husband Tom and ask him to put a lock on the medicine cabinet, which thankfully he did. Tricia and I had keys and we made sure that Joan never got her hands on them. Tom used to come round and take Kitty out for drives every now and then but after a while that stopped, because every time he arrived it would end up in a screaming match between the two of them in front of their little girl and it wasn't good for anyone.

We worked like Trojans for about a year, saving as much of our wages as we could. We even managed to get enough money together to head over to Spain for a week, our first ever holiday abroad and the first time Tricia had been on a plane. We had a ball. Later that year we decided that we would go home for Christmas but we knew that we would need some extra money if we were to go as the job did not pay all that well. We were earning around nine pounds a week and as we liked going out and buying clothes we knew we would not have enough money to go home for the Christmas break. Tricia was really desperate to see her mother as she worried a lot about her.

So one afternoon we sat in the kitchen contemplating what to do to bring in extra cash. We decided that we would both take up some sort of evening work. We knew it would have to be something flexible, as we wouldn't be able to do it every evening. We also wanted something together. After about an hour of going through everything we could think of I suggested that we could do some bar work a few nights a week. Tricia was a bit sceptical because we had no experience, but I knew that we could pull it off. How hard could it be pulling pints and serving tables? I told her that if they asked us about experience we would just say that we had worked in a bar back home.

There were just two minor problems: neither of us had a clue about all the different sorts of drinks available; and Tricia was worried because she couldn't count very well, so giving out change could be a problem for her. But I told her that we could bluff our way through anything once we got ourselves behind a bar. I would make sure that we got that far.

Tricia went along with the idea because she genuinely didn't think we had any chance of getting work in a pub. As soon as she went up to her room, though, my head started to race and I made a decision that my goal for that week would be to get us jobs behind a bar.

I picked up the phone book and began to scan down the pages to find the closest pubs to where we lived. I wrote down those that I thought would suit us best, and of course my preference was for an Irish pub. I made dozens of calls and most of them wanted bar people. Unfortunately as soon as I said there were two of us and we wanted to work together I got a negative response. Most places were only looking for one person and there was no way either of us wanted to go it alone. We had always done things together and it wasn't going to stop now. All we had in this strange country was each other and we had to stick together, no matter what.

I told all the publicans that we were very experienced having worked in pubs in Ireland. Eventually I struck it lucky. A pub that I'll call The Irish Tavern was hiring two bar people and I just happened to ring at the right time. Without even organising an interview to see what we were like, the man on the phone simply asked me when we could start – and that was that. So two nights later we headed into the Irish Tavern to start our new jobs as barmaids.

Little did we know that our part time jobs would change our lives forever.

* * *

The Irish Tavern was in the heart of Ealing Broadway. It was a big and very busy pub. It had three bars – the public one which was the hangout for all the hard-core workers like builders and road workers; the saloon bar for all the office people in their smart suits; and then there was what we called the snug. The snug was very small, an area where customers went to have a quiet drink alone or with a friend. I'm sure many a couple who popped into the snug wanted to be somewhere they could not be seen, and I know for a fact that there were quite a few snug regulars who weren't snuggled up beside their partners. There was many an illicit snog in the snug!

Arnie and Mavis were the managers of the Tavern. Arnie was in his forties and he was going bald but, God love him, he was always trying desperately to make his little bit of hair stretch across the top of his head with a comb-over. His thick glasses didn't do him any justice either. Mavis was quite small. She also wore glasses and had a bob hairstyle that didn't suit her. I think she was a bit wary of Tricia and me – especially when she saw the look on Arnie's face when we walked in the door and told them who we were.

Tricia and I had come to the conclusion that what we lacked in bar experience we made up for in looks, so we decided to play on that. On that first night in the Tavern we dressed up to the nines and we both looked a million dollars, even if I say so myself. I wore a red tartan miniskirt with a white blouse (honestly, they were really in fashion at that time!). I was gifted with an ample bosom, so my blouse bulged a bit and of course my cleavage was on view for all to see. Tricia wore a lovely black miniskirt with a cream top. She had a lovely figure and with her short dark wavy hair everything she wore looked good on her.

So when we walked into the bar and told Arnie who we were his eyes nearly popped out of his head. Mavis spotted his reaction and she quickly took over. She told us what to do and how to use the till and then they both left us alone at the bar to get on with it. We were shocked that they didn't hang around to see how we got on but my spiel on the phone must have convinced them that we were perfect for the job and didn't require any help. Of course, nothing could have been further from the truth.

Thankfully for us it was very quiet that first night and not a lot of people were in the bar, so we just started to familiarise ourselves with all the different bottles of beer and the various spirits that were on the shelves. I remember looking at Tricia and asking, "Do you really think we can do this?" I was beginning to think that we had bitten off more than we could chew.

Surprisingly, she was the one who turned around and said, "Well, if we don't, at least we will have fun trying!" That was good enough for me.

Gradually the pub started to fill up and most people were just asking for bottles, so we were doing all right until one man asked me for a Black 'n' Tan. I had never heard of it so I started to search around on the bottle shelf. I couldn't go back and ask the man what a Black 'n' Tan was, so I was starting to panic. All of a sudden, one of the customers, whom I had noticed earlier as I had served him a pint of lager, called me over and said, "Ann, a Black 'n' Tan is a Guinness and bitter." He told me it was a half pint of draught bitter with a bottle of Guinness. I was mortified but grateful for his help. I served the poor man, who had been waiting for ages at this stage, his Black 'n' Tan and then I went back over to thank the other man for his help.

He was very friendly and said that I could ask him for

help anytime if I was stuck on a drink. True to his word, he did. Danny Moran turned out to be my knight in shining armour. I learned from Danny every drink from an Advocat to a Snowball and what he told me, I told Tricia. So that was how we both became barmaids – and bloody good ones at that, even if I say so myself!

At the weekends there was live music in the pub and the place used to be packed, so there was always extra staff brought in on these nights, mostly men. Tricia and I used to eye them up, but we didn't really fancy any of them. However, there was one fellow who did grab my attention. I had served him as a customer and he was now working behind the bar. The reason he stood out in my mind was that I had thrown a pint of Guinness over his brother one night. He had been annoying the hell out of me, telling me that I wasn't pouring the Guinness properly, so in response to his moaning I got a glass, very carefully and with great precision pulled the pint of black, and then poured it over his head, asking him if that particular one was to his liking. So his brother remembered me only too well. But he obviously took it in good heart because he always had a smile for me and I knew he liked me. We didn't talk that much but it was obvious that there was something there.

One night while we were working the same shift he asked me my name. It was odd because we had been working together for a while but we were both in different areas so we didn't really need to know each other's name. I told him that my name was Ann and he said his was Bobby – and that was that really. We got on with what we had been doing and nothing more was said. Later that night the phone in the passageway rang and as I was the nearest to it I went to answer it. There was a woman on the line and she asked to speak to Liam. I didn't know who she was talking about but she said he worked behind the bar. There were six lads behind the bar, so I asked her to describe this Liam to me. I left the phone hanging and went up to the guy she had described.

"If your name is Bobby," I said, "well, you're not wanted on the phone, but if your name is Liam, then it's for you."

I walked away from him thinking what an idiot he was, telling me his name was Bobby. I made a conscious decision to keep away from him as I could not understand why he would have lied about his name.

On the odd occasion midweek I would work a different shift to Tricia; it didn't happen often but when it did I would have no choice but to go in when she was off. It was normally quiet on weeknights and there would only be a few of the regulars in and a few lads from the local bikers' club, who at times used to take over the public bar. They would come into the pub in a group, sit in the corner and smoke dope most of the evening. The air would be filled with the smell and you'd be inclined to get high on the aroma.

One of the bikers, Stuart, had taken a very keen interest in me but I never led him to believe that I had any feelings for him. He just wasn't my type at all. But he was very persistent; every night he would come into the pub and spend most of his drinking time trying to persuade me to go out with him. It was getting to the stage that he would simply not take "no" for an answer.

One night when I was working on my own he was being

more annoying than ever; he just wasn't letting up. As the night went on, the more he drank the worse he got. There was no talking to him, no way of convincing him that "no" meant "no". He waited until last drinks were served and he said that he would wait outside until I was finished and we could go for a meal.

As the place started to clear I began to get worried. I had no intention of going for a meal with him, but I didn't know what to do to get out of it. He hung around with the other bikers and I knew that if he was outside and there was a gang of them it would be very hard for me to say I didn't want to go. I didn't want to get into a situation like that on my own. So I was in a dilemma trying to figure out the best and most peaceful way to get out of the situation.

The only other person working that night was the guy with the identity crisis – the one who wasn't sure if he was Bobby or Liam. I had no other choice but to ask him if he would walk me up to the taxi rank when we finished cleaning up. I explained why I needed his help and I was relieved when he said that he would.

It turned out that I didn't have to worry at all, because when we got outside there was no sign of Stuart. Not a biker in sight. But he continued to walk me to the taxi rank. There wasn't a cab in sight, so we ended up going for a coffee to kill a bit of time. There was a Wimpy bar right across the road from the taxi rank. Two hours later, having got to know Liam and found him to be a very decent man, and having arranged to meet him again, I finally got my taxi home.

* * *

I started to go out with Liam Kenny a few nights a week. Everything went fine at first, but there were times when he wouldn't turn up after arranging a date. This happened quite a lot so I learnt quickly not to let it get to me. When he failed to turn up I would simply take myself off to the Hibernia Dance Hall in Fulham, as I had made a pact with myself never to hang around waiting on any man. He would always ring the next day with an excuse that he had been working late, as he worked on the building sites as well as in the pub, and I always believed him.

Some months after I had started to see Liam, Joan decided to put the care home up for sale and move back to Ireland, as things were not working out as well as she had wanted. She was finding it very difficult to bring up two children and run the home so soon after giving birth. It was a tough decision for her because I know she loved her work. But it was even worse for Tricia and myself because it meant that we would soon be out of our jobs. The bigger problem for us was that we would also be out of our home, with nowhere to live and no money to pay rent.

We liked our jobs and we had got on very well with the old people living there. They were all very upset as well at how things had worked out and their families were forced to find alternative accommodation for them. Joan helped them out as much as possible, using her contacts with other nursing homes in the area, many of which were very willing to take in more residents. But it was a big upheaval for the old folk, as they were well and truly settled in at the home and they had all become close friends. It was like one big happy family. But these things happen and you just have to get on with it.

Tricia and I asked around in the pub to see if anyone knew of any reasonable digs in the area that could take the two of us. We were put in touch with someone who knew someone else who happened to have a room to let in south Ealing. Because we were really desperate for somewhere to live in a hurry, we took this room – much to our regret, as it was the filthiest room I had ever come across. I don't think it even had a kitchen. The bedding was disgusting, as were the toilet and separate bathroom. Tricia and I bought new bed linen and painted the room, but we had to leave after about two weeks as we both got ill with all the damp.

Tricia had been in a relationship for a while with a lovely guy called Mick, so she moved in with him, which left me on my own. Although I was seeing Liam I didn't want to live with him yet, so I found myself a room with a family and got Tricia and myself a job in a clothes factory on the Great West Road. We also continued with the bar work to pull in a bit of extra money.

After a few months Liam asked me if we could get a place together as he was living with his sister and she had three young children. So I gave in and we found a place in Greenford. Our landlady and her husband were both from Ireland. She was paralysed and confined to a wheelchair and her husband had to do most of the fetching and carrying. She was very abusive to him and most nights we would hear them screaming and shouting at each other. In fact some nights they were so rowdy you would have sworn they were in the same room as us. She cursed at him all the time and she didn't seem to give him a minute to himself.

Thankfully, as we had our own keys to the front door and

we got a key to our room, we didn't have to meet either of them very often, except on a Saturday morning when the husband would call up to collect the rent money. I always let Liam deal with him as I didn't like either of them and I wanted as little as possible to do with them. I was still working at the clothes factory at this time but I had changed pubs and I was now working in a pub that I'll call The Bell, in Southall.

* * *

My relationship with Liam was going well at this time, although I did feel that he was spending too much time with his mates in the pub. He said it was because I was working most evenings and he didn't want to sit indoors on his own. But we got through our little ups and downs, like every other couple, and we carried on.

When we had been living together for about a year I found out I was pregnant and Liam asked me to marry him. I had gone to the doctor as I had missed a period and wasn't feeling well. I nearly died when he told me that the test was positive. I was terrified of being labelled like every other young girl who became pregnant outside marriage, but not for one minute did I consider giving my child away. No matter what, I was going to give this child all the love that I had never known, and more.

But I wasn't sure if I wanted to get married. I explained to Liam that I did not want him in later years to throw back in my face that he had only married me because I was pregnant. He said that he would never do such a thing, and he never did.

So I agreed to marry him and we started to make the arrangements for the big day. We didn't have too much time to spare. I knew it wouldn't be long before I started to show and I didn't want to be saying "I Do" with a big bump sticking out from under the dress.

We went to a local church and spoke to the priest, who was not at all impressed with the fact that I was pregnant. However, he agreed to overlook the situation and marry us. We set a date for the 30th of March 1974.

When I was sending out the invitations I decided to send one to mother and father. Their response was much as I should have expected – a note to say that they wouldn't be able to make it over for the wedding. No excuses, no lies to cover up the embarrassment of refusing, seeing that they had reared me as my "parents". They never sent congratulations, asked who I was marrying, how I had met him, where he was from . . . nothing. No, they just said they couldn't make it. I was upset but I decided to put it all out of my head and get on with the preparations for the wedding. I had enough to worry about.

I didn't dare tell my mother that I was pregnant as I felt that she would have had a field day if she knew. So I just put all my effort into arranging my big day and preparing for the arrival of my baby. I knew in my heart that I really had no family. The response of my so-called parents just confirmed that, so there was no point in worrying. I just had to get on with my life and forget about the people in my past. And that was what I was going to do.

CHAPTER SEVEN

Married Life

I had many doubts about my up-and-coming marriage. The closer it came to the day, the worse I got. I was very, very tired as well because I was pregnant, working and trying to organise everything for the big day on my own. Tricia was a great help and I don't know what I would have done without her.

We had invited around sixty or seventy people from Ireland and England to celebrate with us. Liam's mother and sister were coming from their hometown in Ulster but his dad couldn't make it; I'm not sure why. Liam had another sister living in London and she had agreed to come up with her husband as well. It was going to be very strange for me because I had never met his mother. The thoughts of meeting her just before I married her son was a bit nerve-racking, but I had no choice in the matter.

To top it all, I wasn't even sure if I wanted to go through with it myself. I asked myself the question over and over again. *Was* I marrying Liam simply because we had a baby on the way? I had left my hometown to avoid a situation like that and here I was in London in that very situation. Admittedly, most of the girls I knew back home were a lot worse off, as the men were often a lot older than them – old farmers who loved having their way with the local pretty young things. It was sick. I was lucky that I hadn't found myself in their position. But I also thought about the "what ifs" – what if mother heard I was pregnant and hadn't got married? I could almost hear her voice: "I told you so – sure what would you expect from a bastard? Like mother, like daughter." She was so predictable. And what if I decided not to walk up the aisle? What kind of a life would my unborn child have without their father? I had to think of him or her as well. I also wasn't a hundred per cent sure if I loved Liam, and if it was "me" that was marrying for the wrong reason. I kept asking myself if I would marry Liam if I wasn't pregnant, and I kept coming up with the same answer. I knew if I didn't get married I would be just like my mother and I didn't want that. I was going to keep quiet about how I was really feeling. For all the wrong reasons I was going to walk up the aisle to take my vows.

My head was wrecked. I was all over the place. And there was another thing playing on my mind, which I hadn't even mentioned to Tricia. It was something that had really affected me, foolishly maybe, but it was still worrying me. A few weeks before our wedding, Liam changed job and went to work in another pub a short distance away from where we were staying. He tended to chop and change jobs quite a bit, but this time he was running the place and he saw it as a big challenge that he would really enjoy. I went in to see him one morning before opening time. As I walked in the door he was stocking up the shelves behind the bar. The jukebox was playing. I stopped dead in my tracks when I heard the song that he had chosen to play. It was called *Shot Gun Wedding* and the lyrics were just a bit too close to the bone for me.

Now you may think I was being paranoid, but knowing that he had purposely picked out that song from a whole range on the jukebox freaked me out. I was having doubts already so I immediately thought, *This guy is obviously only marrying me because he thinks he has to, just to avoid any embarrassment or out of some kind of guilt.* He saw the shocked look on my face and it registered with him, so I asked him straight out, "Is that how you actually feel?" Of course he told me he only chose that song because he liked it. But it seemed very odd to me and I couldn't get the lyrics out of my head for days. I decided not to mention it again.

* * *

When the wedding day finally came around we were running here and there like headless chickens trying to organise things. That morning Tricia and I went to the hairdressers in Ealing to get all spruced up. Tricia was, of course, my bridesmaid. When we came out of the hairdressers I had intended to walk back to the bedsit – it was only five minutes away – but instead I found myself getting on a bus heading for Shepherd's Bush – the opposite direction to where I lived. I hadn't even thought about it – I just saw the bus coming up the road and thought I'd get on. There must have been something at the back of my head telling me to run, because although I was putting on a brave face I was genuinely worried about Liam's drinking and whether or not I could cope with it.

I was in a bit of a daze but I could hear Tricia shouting as she ran after me to get on the bus, "What the hell are you doing? You're getting married in an hour's time! You can't just run off – everyone will be there waiting on you to arrive!" The bus was still stopped as the driver waited on the rest of the people to board. For a split second I came back to reality and jumped onto the footpath. I decided that I couldn't leave everyone standing there waiting. I had made my choice and I had no other option now but to go through with it.

Tricia knew that I was a bundle of nerves but I think she suspected it was the usual last minute jitters, not a genuine fear of what may lie ahead. We headed back to the house and started to get dressed. Just a few minutes after we closed the front door, there was a knock and standing there was our best man Paddy holding a bunch of flowers. I shouted down to ask if Liam was with him because I knew Paddy wouldn't be there on his own. He told me he wasn't but, when I peeked out the window sure enough there was my husband-to-be standing beside the car having a cigarette. So I asked Paddy if Liam thought I wasn't going to turn up. I knew he was checking up on me in case I made a show of him by not walking down the aisle. To this day I don't know if he had seen me getting onto that bus heading in the opposite direction or he had just genuinely had a bad feeling – but something made him come to the house that day to check up on me. We never spoke about it in all the years we were married. The lads drove off and Tricia and I put the final touches to the dress and make-up.

I wore a borrowed wedding dress and I had the customary garter, in baby blue. One of our friends Mick, who had a lovely red Jaguar car, drove me to the church. He knew that red was my favourite colour so he decked the car out in lots of red and pink ribbons and I had pink carnations in my bouquet. As we headed out the door I looked in the mirror, turned to Tricia and said, "Well, there's no going back now." I could see that she was really concerned but I told her that I was fine and we headed off to the church. How could I tell her that I felt sick, scared and worried and that my nerves were shattered?

So I left that small bedsit as a single (albeit pregnant) woman, knowing I would be coming back to it as a pregnant but married one. I took one last look at the clock as I rushed out the door and realised that I was already more than half an hour late for the church, but I wasn't bothered – at least I was turning up. When we finally got to the churchyard, poor Paddy was pacing the footpath with sweat running down his brow. He shouted at me, "What the hell kept you?"

"I was just enjoying my last few moments of being single," I told him.

He looked at me as if I was mad. "Liam was getting worried – he thought something might have happened to you."

I knew Liam was only worrying in case I had done a runner.

I walked up to Neil, who was a good friend to both of us. He had offered to walk me down the aisle when we first decided to tie the knot, as I had nobody else to hand me over to my new husband. I could see Liam at the front of the church as he turned with a big grin on his face to watch me walk down the aisle. I thought he looked very smart in his brown pinstripe suit. But as I approached him I could hear a voice in my head asking, *what are you doing here?* But I chose to ignore the warning voice and I continued to walk down the aisle to take my vows – for better or worse, for richer or poorer, in sickness and in health, to love, honour and obey until death do us part.

I had no idea then just how those words would haunt me for the rest of my life.

* * *

Despite the jitters, we had a good day and everyone enjoyed the meal and the music. We began married life back at the bedsit – no honeymoon for us.

I continued to work in the clothes factory until I was eight months' pregnant. The boss was a man called Tom who was very kind and I got on well with him. He didn't have to keep me on when he found out I was pregnant because he would have found someone else to fill my place quite easily, someone who could stand all day like I had to at that time. It was a small factory and we made school uniforms, but we always seemed to be busy, not just during the summer months. But Tom was very understanding and he told me that he would give me an easy job that would not entail heavy work. He gave me a position pressing buttons onto clothing all day. I was very lucky. On an easy day I could just sit at my machine and daydream. Tom allowed us to keep the radio on while we worked and we would all sing along, especially when "Seasons in the-Sun" by Terry Jacks came on.

I was attending the doctor and the hospital quite regularly by now and my boss didn't have any problem with me heading off whenever I needed to. Most days the appointments were after work but the odd time I would have to go in the afternoon. I would take my doctor's notes into work with me and then head off in the afternoon.

One day I came into work without the notes and I only realised it as I went back to my desk after morning break. I knew that I could make it back to the house in time at lunchtime if I left a few minutes earlier. One of my friends came with me. When we arrived back at the flat and went upstairs to my room I got the shock of my life. There was someone in my room rummaging around. I nearly passed out on the spot. When they turned around I got an even bigger surprise. I thought I was witnessing a miracle. It was my landlady – the same one that was supposed to be paralysed and confined to a wheelchair. There she was, as large as life, walking around my room, not a wheelchair or a walking stick in sight.

"What the bloody hell are you doing in my room?" I shouted. "And how in the name of God did you get up here? You are supposed to be crippled."

At first she looked as though she was frozen to the spot and was lost for words, but it didn't take her long to find her tongue. She launched at me with a tirade of foul language: "It's my bloody house and I have the right to come into the room if I want to!" With that she marched out of the room and down the stairs.

I stood there with my mouth open. I couldn't think of what to say or do. My friend said not to do anything, to leave it to Liam and let him deal with it when he came in that evening. I knew she was right but I kept wondering if he would believe what had happened. And if he did, would he completely lose the plot and go ballistic?

I went ahead and told him that evening. He went downstairs and there was an almighty row. It all came out in the wash; we found that the situation was worse than we had thought. It hadn't been a one-off miracle trip upstairs for our landlady. It seemed that they were both regularly coming into our room when we were out, her to have a nose around the place and him to rob the cash from the gas meter in the room. The next day we went out and bought our own lock for the door, but I never felt comfortable there after that incident. I always looked around after work for signs that anything had been disturbed.

* * *

Throughout my pregnancy I had shared care between my own GP and the hospital. The doctor had told me that the baby was due on the 18th of July and the hospital told me I was due in August. So between the two of them I didn't know where I was. In my own mind the July date seemed to be spot on, so I was going by that.

During one of the hospital appointments the consultant, whom I hadn't met before, told me that I was in labour. This was great news to me, but the doctor didn't want me to go into labour at that time. During the course of my pregnancy I had to have a lot of tests carried out as the baby was not growing as well as expected and they wanted to find out why. It was during these tests that they discovered my womb was actually split in two and that the baby was growing on one side of the womb. They also discovered that my cervix was damaged and if I was to give birth naturally there was a strong possibility that my baby could die and the birth could also put my own life at risk. I would therefore have to have a caesarean.

I was admitted immediately. The obstetric team came in and out all day and they poked and prodded me. I was feeling very anxious and getting depressed; this was my first pregnancy and I was totally green about what to expect. I was put in a ward with a lot of other women all going through the stages of labour before being moved to the delivery room. I lay there wondering what was going to happen to me.

Things were moving very slowly and I was bored silly. I just wanted to have my baby and go home. The doctor was doing his rounds in the late afternoon and when he came to my bed he asked me how often the contractions were coming. Just for something to say, and so they would leave me alone, I told him they were coming every five minutes. Of course, I hadn't got a clue what I was talking about!

He told the nurse to get me ready and with that he walked away. As they were leaving I called the nurse back. "What am I supposed to be getting ready for?"

"What do you mean? You are in labour, aren't you?"

"Well, they keep telling me that I'm in labour and I'm supposed to be getting some kind of pains, but I'm not," I said, before adding, "I told the doctor I had them every five minutes because I just wanted him to leave me alone."

She was panicking now because the doctor had told her to prepare me and yet here I was saying I was fine. The poor woman didn't know what to believe.

Later that evening I was moved to another ward to await the birth – operation cancelled. I'm sure they were really pissed off at me but the doctor had said I was in labour and they couldn't risk letting me out, even though I felt fine.

In the end, I was kept in hospital for a week to be monitored.

* * *

Finally, on the 10th of July, our beautiful daughter, our firstborn, Sarah, came into the world, weighing 5lb 3oz.

She had some kind of breathing problem and was given just twelve hours to live, but she had other ideas. She was kept in an incubator in the ICU for a week.

To make matters worse, I didn't recover well after the birth, and I didn't get to see my little baby for the first three days of her life. I felt awful, because those few days are meant to be crucial for a mother and baby to bond, but there was absolutely nothing I could do. It was all out of my control.

Liam spent a lot of time up in ICU with Sarah and then he would pop down to see me. I would live for him coming in because I relied on him to keep me posted on her progress. It was very hard for me not being there for my little child after carrying her around inside my body for nine whole months. There is no point in people saying to a new mum who has been separated from her baby that she and the baby will have the rest of their lives ahead of them to bond – every mother wants to be with her baby all day, every day, once it arrives into the world.

When they eventually took me up to see Sarah I was terrified to touch her as she looked so tiny. I was frightened of all the wires and machines connected to her, which were making strange beeping sounds.

But she was our little miracle baby. She defied all the odds and after a week hooked up to machines they told us that we could take her out of the incubator and give her a proper hug. Unfortunately I was still not allowed to bring her down to the ward to be with me because of the risk of infection. I spent most of my days with her, sitting beside the plastic cot, watching and praying, and staring at every little feature on her tiny body.

One morning when I went up to see Sarah I walked in to find the doctor standing beside her crib. I panicked, thinking that something had happened to her while I was away, but as soon as he saw the look on my face he reassured me that everything was fine. He was just about to give her an injection so I had come at the right time to comfort her when she cried. I had never heard my baby cry in all the time I had sat with her and I was really looking forward to hearing her little voice screech for the first time. But my beautiful little baby never batted an eyelid when she got her injections; she simply took it all in her stride. The doctor said that she had probably got used to them as the poor little thing was having roughly seven injections a day. Her tiny heel was covered in white sticky tape from the numerous injections and blood tests she had received in the first few days of her life.

As I was laying my little girl back in her cot and tucking her in, the doctor asked me if I liked surprises: "You can take her back to the ward with you today." I didn't know whether to laugh or cry. I was so overcome. To think that at last I could have her with me and that Liam's family could come and see her, as only myself and Liam had been allowed in the ICU ward.

However, there was one condition. Sarah had to go back to the ICU at night. I couldn't keep her beside me at night because they needed to keep her monitored while I slept. But this didn't bother me – I was just delighted that I would finally be like all the other mothers in the ward, able to cuddle my tiny little miracle in my arms, bathe her, feed her and dress her like a little doll.

As soon as I got back to the ward I rang Liam to tell him the good news. Because I was so excited I told him to tell everyone that if they wanted to come in they could. Visiting time that day was both exciting and tiring. A lot of Liam's family came in laden down with presents for the baby and flowers and chocolates for me. I was exhausted by the time they had all left but our little bundle just lay there, not a bother on her. Sarah was the perfect host because there wasn't a murmur out of her despite everyone pulling and tugging at her.

When they had all left I decided to put her into one of the babygros that they had brought in. She had been wearing the standard hospital one since she arrived into the world and now I wanted to dress her up in some of the lovely presents I had received. She looked and smelt absolutely gorgeous. As I was doing this the other women in the ward came over to speak to me and to see the baby, all except one lady whom I had noticed across the room from me. She'd had a baby boy two days before this and I heard her say to one of the nurses that it was her fourth boy. To me she looked too young to have four children, but at visiting time on the day her baby was born, her husband had come in with the other three boys and they had spent the time running under all the beds in the ward.

I didn't know why she hadn't come over when the other women came. I asked her, "Are you all right?"

"I'm fine," she said. Then she added, "You had a lot of visitors today."

"Well, it's their first time to see the baby because she's been in ICU for a week."

"Ah, I'd wondered what had happened," she said. "I thought maybe you had lost her."

"No, and she's perfect now. I'm just happy to have her with me."

We left it at that and I thought nothing more about it.

At about nine o'clock that evening, Linda, the woman who was in the bed beside mine, asked me if I would go down to the dayroom with her as she wanted to have a cigarette. I checked the baby to make sure she was nice and cosy and we headed off. But halfway down the corridor I decided to go back and bring the baby to the nursery just in case she cried when I wasn't there. I told Linda I would follow her down to the dayroom as soon as I got her settled.

I strolled back to the ward. As I came into the room I saw that there was a light on over my bed. I assumed that one of the nurses was checking on the baby. When I drew the curtain back I got the shock of my life. The woman across the ward – the mother of four boys – had taken Sarah out of her cot and had put her baby son into it instead. She had put all the clothes that I had got for the baby that day in a carrier bag and had my baby wrapped up in a blanket. It looked like she was ready to leave the hospital with her.

I screamed at the top of my voice. I had a horrible feeling of being stuck to the ground, unable to move. Suddenly my bed was surrounded by patients and nurses. The next thing I remember is the floor coming up to meet me. I collapsed in a heap and was unconscious for ages.

Looking back on it years later I think they must have sedated me. When I woke up there was a nurse sitting beside my bed, watching over me. I went into a big panic over my little girl. I was terrified in case that woman had done something to her. I sat up in the bed, absolutely shaking with fear, and I asked the nurse where my baby was.

"Your baby is fine," she told me. "She is back upstairs in the ICU ward. The doctor decided that she should stay there tonight."

I begged her to let me see her to make sure that she was fine and she took me up without another word. I'm sure she knew how frantic I was with worry. When we went up to the ICU I was so relieved to see Sarah. I asked the nurse, "What happened? Where is that woman now?" I had noticed on our way out of the ward that the bed across from me was empty.

The nurse told me, "The police have taken her away for questioning. Don't worry, everything is going to be fine."

I was in still in shock. I kept asking, over and over, "Why did she want my baby?"

She looked at me kindly. "You had a little girl and she wanted a little girl but she had another boy instead. She is very depressed and she thought that by swapping the baby around she would be well gone before you got back. Luckily for you, you came back and caught her."

Liam and myself were just grateful that we had Sarah back safely in our arms. Thankfully we all came through our ordeal unscathed and two weeks later we both went home to our little bedsit.

Nothing more was ever done or said about the near-abduction. Back then you just accepted things. There was no such thing as going to the papers or suing the hospital. I didn't even have a counsellor allocated to talk to me. Life just went on. To this day when I see cases of abduction on the news, I cringe at the thought that it could have been me.

* * *

I was home about a week when I started to haemorrhage very badly. Liam was at work when it happened but I managed with some effort to contact my doctor who said that he would phone an ambulance and that he would be with me as soon as he could. I also called Liam's sister who came to look after the baby. When the doctor arrived he gave me an injection.

While the ambulance men were helping me into the back of the ambulance, the doctor went over to talk to my sister-in-law about the baby and then he stopped to chat with the landlady. When he got into the ambulance, he said, "You don't have a very nice landlady. Do you want to know what she said to me?"

Of course, I was dying to know. He said, "She told me that the bleeding was caused by your husband having sex with you. She said that he couldn't wait for the six weeks' recovery period and that he forced you to have sex."

I nearly died. I sat straight up and said "That's a horrible lie." Then I asked him, "What do you think is wrong with me? Am I going to bleed to death?"

"No, Ann, you're not going to die. I think they may have left half of the afterbirth inside you. We need to get to the hospital as fast as possible so they can get it sorted out."

So I was admitted back into the hospital once again and after a little operation I was eventually allowed home. However, I had plenty of time to think when I was in that hospital bed. I decided that I was not going back to the bedsit. I could not bear to be in the same house as that woman again. So we went to stay with Liam's sister in Southall until we found a place.

After a few weeks and long searching through the "to let" pages of the local papers we eventually found a place that we liked. There was only one drawback – for a reduced rent

I would have to take care of the landlady, as she had suffered a stroke. I decided to go and see her when her daughter would be there and make my decision based on that visit. I explained to them that I had a very small baby and they said that would not be a problem. So, after agreeing a rent of five pounds a week, Liam, myself and our new baby moved into the house a few days later. I was so happy to leave that mad woman in the bedsit. It was like a weight had been lifted off my shoulders.

Mrs Hall was a lovely woman but had got very depressed after her stroke and was sometimes very bitter. Despite this, we got on very well and she loved having the baby around. She went to a care centre during the day, which meant that I had time to do what I wanted for a few hours a day. Generally this arrangement worked very well and everything was rosy.

Or so I thought.

* * *

After about six months I noticed that Liam was sometimes not coming home in the evenings until very late, as he would go to the pub after work with the lads. We had quite a few rows over this as I thought that he should at least come home and see his little baby before she went to bed for the night. He would do so for a week or two to keep the peace but it soon reverted back to the late evenings. Unfortunately it got even worse when he got a job in the Halfway House pub. He worked nearly every night – or so he told me. What I couldn't understand was, if he worked every night, why then were we still struggling to pay the rent and the bills? I wasn't earning any money and so I was totally dependent on him. I hated asking him every week for housekeeping money. It was a total nightmare. He would scream and shout at me and tell me that I didn't deserve any money as I was doing nothing all day but just "sitting on my arse". He didn't for one minute think, of course, that I was the one looking after his daughter, and I also had Mrs Hall to look after as well.

He made me feel awful, screaming all sorts of comments at me about how I looked and how the house looked. I made a solemn vow to myself that I would always be dressed nicely when he came home each evening. I would also have a clean house and a meal cooked every night and most of all I would not nag him about not coming home early. I didn't want any more hassle so I also decided that in future I would wait for him to give me the housekeeping money instead of me always asking for it.

I tried this method for a few weeks but that didn't work either. If I didn't ask for housekeeping money he wouldn't give it. Also, trying to keep calm every time he came in late was getting harder and harder.

One night when he came home I noticed that he was not his usual self. He was full of the joys of spring. I knew something was up. I asked him what was going on and he said that we were going to run a pub back in Ireland.

I was disgusted with him for even thinking about something like that, let alone organising it, without even talking to me. I thought to myself: *Am I hearing right? Did he just say that we were going back to Ireland? When was all this arranged?* He proceeded to tell me about a friend of the landlord in the pub where he worked, who was looking for someone to run his pub in a little town in Northern Ireland. Liam told this man that he would love to do it – without saying a word to me or thinking about his family.

"What about what I want?" I shouted. "Did you even bother to think about that? I am fuming that this deal was signed, sealed and delivered without asking me."

He turned the tables on me, trying to make me feel guilty. "I thought you'd have been happy for me," he said.

I turned on him immediately. "Happy for you, why should I be happy for you? I think, Liam, you are missing the point here. This is not about you. Have you forgotten that we have a child to consider? What about her?"

He started to get moody and aggressive. "Well, we're going back whether you like it or not, so you'd better start getting used to the idea." With that he stormed out of the room and went to bed.

I knew that there was no use in continuing with the subject because he had already made his mind up and there was no way in the world that I or anyone else was going to change it that night anyway. So, the next morning, when he had calmed down and sobered up, I asked him, "Are you really serious about going to Ireland to run a pub?"

"Yes. It's all arranged. We're all heading off in two weeks, and that's that."

I could see there was no turning him now. "What are we going to do about poor Mrs Hall? I feel really bad about leaving her alone and without much notice." But it was obvious that he couldn't have cared less about her. All he was concerned about was himself, no one else mattered.

He got up without saying a word and walked away. Because that's what Liam did when he didn't want to deal with things. He would walk away from the problem, whatever it was, and leave the shit for someone else to clear up.

I was very depressed about the whole situation. I had settled in nicely with Mrs Hall and I had really grown close to her and her to me. She trusted me and she loved having a baby around the house. And now Liam was dragging me away kicking and screaming, with not a care in the world for me, our baby or anyone else. I didn't know how I was going to break the news to Mrs Hall. I knew that she would be devastated. I had also recently arranged for her to go to a day centre for three days a week. She loved it and I was getting a bit of a breather, which meant that I could spend more time with the baby and meet up on the odd occasion with some friends for a cuppa and a chat.

Now not only was I going to have to tell her that I was leaving her in the lurch, I was also going to have to leave all of my friends behind as well, especially Tricia. She too had got married and was expecting her first baby. I wanted to be there for her, both during and after the birth of her baby, as a support. I was also worried about Mrs Hall, though, because I knew that sometimes she let things get to her. When I broke the news, I could see that she was shocked. She had become so dependent on me and now she would be on her own again. I could see the hurt and fear in her eyes but I explained to her that it was out of my hands and that if I had my way I wouldn't be going anywhere. She seemed calm after that, probably because she knew that the decision was made and there was nothing that any of us could do about it.

As the days went by and I got used to the idea of moving again I began to think that it may not be a bad idea after all. I had noticed that Liam was drinking even more than ever now. Not only was he coming home in a heap but he was getting very argumentative. I couldn't say "boo" to him without him starting a row. This was a side that I had not seen before we were married. So I began to think that getting away from his drinking pals could be a blessing. In truth, I may have been fooling myself and simply convinced myself that everything would be different if we moved away from the situation. I think this was because I had been controlled all of my life and it was very hard for me to stand up for myself. I could only go so far and then I'd pull back simply to keep the peace.

One way or another, we were going. I spent the next week or so trying to get everything ready. I was still left very much in the dark about which pub we were going to. All Liam would say every time I asked him about it was, "Don't worry". Of course I worried! This was a big thing for me. I was going back to Ireland after waiting twenty-one years to get out of it. It may not have been the same county, but it was nearly as good as. It was all right for him. He was going to be grand, as he would have all of his family around him, because the pub was only a couple of hours' drive away from his parents' house. But what about me? Did anyone care? I knew that I had no other choice in the matter. I was married to this man and he wanted more than anything to go home. So I reluctantly agreed, mainly to keep Liam happy, and I hoped that maybe within one of his brainwaves there might lie a miracle that would make him see sense and change some of his bad ways,

We would be travelling with a guy called Andy who owned a pub in a fairly big town in Ulster. The plan was to drive most of the night up to Stranraer and then take the ferry across to Larne before driving on to our new business venture a couple of hours away from the ferry port. So we packed everything up, bid our farewells and left England. As we drove off into the sunset I had a foreboding feeling that we were doing the wrong thing. But I kept that thought to myself and decided that whatever would be, would be. I prayed that I would be proved wrong.

CHAPTER EIGHT

An Interlude in Hell

I will always remember the morning we arrived in our new home and what my first impressions were of the town and the pub. It was a wet, cold and miserable day. The main street of the town did not look inviting at all; in fact it looked very gloomy and dirty. I looked at the worn-down, decrepit shop fronts, and I thought, *How in God's name am I going to live here?*

The pub we were due to run was right next door to the Court House. It was called The Lake Bar but it was situated on this gloomy street and although it looked fine from the outside the inside was a mess. The first thing that struck me as we walked through the front door was the rotten smell of stale beer and the fact that it mustn't have seen a lick of paint for years. The air hung heavy with the smell of cigarettes.

I had always prided myself on being a good barmaid and I liked to keep things clean and tidy behind the bar, as this is one of the things that landlords were very particular about. Tricia and I would never leave work without making sure that the area behind the bar was spotless. When my foot stuck to the floor as I walked in I knew it was going to be bad – but nothing could have prepared me for what lay ahead.

The pub itself consisted of three bars; to the left there was one very large room that had a dance floor near a stage, with tables and chairs around the walls. It stank of must and looked very drab, with hardly any light coming in through the windows. On the right there was a smaller bar; it was very basic with just tables and chairs around the side. Next to that was another big room with a snooker table. There was a corridor off this room containing the men's toilet and connecting into the other room that held the stage.

As I walked around I began to feel sick; each area I looked at seemed even filthier than the next. The floors were thick with dirt and the shelves holding the glasses were covered in a layer of dust.

Then I happened to come across the kitchen, which was right next to the room with the snooker table. The place was stinking, filthy and covered in grease and grime. When I opened the oven door I screamed at the top of my voice as a dead rat stared up at me, eyes wide open.

I burst into tears in front of Liam and Andy. What had I done, bringing my little girl to a kip like this, just so that her father could live yet another of his doomed dreams? When I calmed down I decided that Liam wasn't man enough to comment on how bad the pub was, so I turned to Andy and said, "We need to talk." No more Mr Nice Guy. "I am disgusted at the state of this place. How long has it been closed down?"

"But it isn't closed at all," he told me.

He could have knocked me sideways – I couldn't believe that people were still drinking and eating in this dive. "Do you mean to tell me that this shithole is still open and people actually come in here to have a drink?"

At this stage I could see he was getting uncomfortable and he stood up and said, "My brother has been running this place for me. I didn't tell him that you were coming, so he doesn't know anything about you being here yet."

Liam and I looked at each other in total disbelief and then back at Andy. I broke the silence. "Are you saying what I think I am hearing? That you have not told your own brother that we were coming here to work for you? What is he going to say when you do tell him?"

He shrugged his shoulders. "I'll sort my brother out. Look, I'm sorry about the state of the place. I'd no idea how much of a dump it had turned into."

He headed off to find his brother, leaving us to have a look around. Liam and I started to have a proper look at the place and we found that the living quarters were as bad as the rest of the place. It looked as though the brother had been storing all the rubbish upstairs, where we were meant to be setting up home.

I told Liam there and then, "This is probably one of your worst mistakes ever. There is no way I'm staying in such a hellhole."

When Andy came back and said that everything was okay with his brother, although I didn't believe him, Liam never opened his mouth to complain about a thing. Once again, I did all the talking. "Andy, we can't run any pub in that condition. If you don't close it up for a week and give us a bit of time to clean it up and paint it, then I'm heading back to England with my baby!"

I could see that he and Liam were shocked at my outburst and even more so when I said, "You obviously care more about the shitty profits you could lose in one week than you do for the future of your pub."

He eventually agreed to close it down and we – well, mostly I – set about cleaning the place up.

* * *

We worked our backs off that week, scrubbing and painting, ordering in stock and trying to make the living area for ourselves as habitable as possible in just a few days. I couldn't believe how we turned it around in such a short time and within weeks the place was hopping. We put up a sign saying "Under New Management" and word got around about the changes in the pub. Soon we were out the door with punters. In fact it was doing so well that we even decided to put on some music at the weekends to raise the profits. Everything was going great and even Liam was behaving himself better than I had expected. There were the usual fights at the end of the night but we always had a few regulars who would jump in and sort things out for us when it got out of hand.

I was starting to enjoy our new venture and I thought things were finally looking up for us.

Then one morning Liam told me that he was thinking of letting out one of the rooms upstairs for meetings. He was being very vague about the whole thing and I couldn't understand why someone would want to use a room over a pub to hold meetings. When I asked who wanted the room he just said, "They do."

"And who, may I ask, are 'they'?"

"The IRA," he muttered.

"You're joking," I said. "When did they ask you this and who exactly asked you?"

He told me that it was one of the guys who came in nearly every lunchtime and every evening. I knew this guy well and liked him because he was always very friendly – but there was no way I would allow the IRA into our home to organise whatever "missions" they were planning.

Liam went on, "He asked me a few days ago. I told him that I'd have to say it to you first before I could give him a yes or a no."

"Thank God you did," I said. "Jesus, Liam, this puts us in a right dilemma."

Stupidly he said, "I don't understand what you mean. What dilemma?"

I looked at him as if he was a complete gobshite. "What are we going to tell them? If we say yes, it will look like we are getting involved and if we say no then it will look like we are anti-IRA and that could really cause us trouble. So whatever answer we give them, we could suffer the consequences."

It was as if a light bulb had suddenly been switched on in his head. "I see what you mean." But instead of sitting down and working this uneasy situation out together he went back to his old ways and walked off to the bar to pour himself a large whiskey.

Over the following days I noticed that his drinking was getting bad again and his behaviour and attitude were no better. He didn't talk about the meeting room for a few days and I didn't bother bringing it up because what I said obviously didn't really matter anyway. He would make up his own mind.

* * *

A few days after our conversation about the IRA I was in the lounge area playing around with the baby. Liam came in and sat down on a stool. I noticed that there was something wrong with him and I asked him if he was all right. He said he was fine and he called Sarah over to him. As she started to run across to him I saw him stumble and shake and he collapsed, banging his head off the floor. I didn't know what was happening to him or how to help him. John, one of the men who worked with us, happened to walk in and ran over to Liam. He shouted at me to get a spoon quickly to put into Liam's mouth to stop him biting his tongue. When I got back Liam was lying very still. I was terrified.

Liam was bleeding from the mouth and there was a bruise on his head. John called an ambulance and Liam was taken to hospital. My mind was racing. John tried to calm me down, saying that everything would be okay and that Liam had taken some kind of fit.

During all of this commotion I had forgotten about Sarah, who I found sitting in the corner of the room crying. I lifted her up and hugged her. "Daddy will be all right," I told her, over and over. I decided to take her to the beach because there was no one else to look after her and I thought it might take her mind off things. I was worried about Liam, but I knew that he was in the best place and there was nothing I could do for him. My first concern was for Sarah. When we got back to the pub a few hours later, I rang the hospital to see how he was. They told me that he was fine, but they were going to keep him in for a few days for some tests. I was more at ease now that I had spoken to the hospital. I also made a decision to get a childminder for Sarah, if only for a couple of hours a day, so that they could take her to the beach and the park.

A few days after Liam went to the hospital, while I was working in the bar at lunchtime, I went over to serve a man standing at the hatch. It wasn't until I was nearly beside him that I realised he was the fellow who had asked my husband about letting the room. I was taken aback for a minute. I hadn't given it any more thought because of Liam's fit. I decided not to say anything about it, unless of course he asked me. He was his usual chatty self, enquiring about Liam and so forth. I was hoping that he had forgotten all about his request. But after about an hour or so he beckoned me to come over to him and asked me, "Has your husband spoken to you about the room?"

My heart was pounding but I stood my ground and said,

"As much as I would like to, I'm afraid I can't. I have my daughter to think about and also Andy would not allow me to let rooms. I am really sorry."

"Not to worry," he said, smiling. "Sure if I hadn't asked I wouldn't have known."

As he walked out the pub door I breathed a sign of relief and prayed that the answer I had given him had satisfied him. I had been caught on the hop and the excuse I gave just came from the top of my head. Andy had never said anything about not letting rooms, but I wasn't going to tell him that. I also had no idea what Liam was going to say to him, if anything.

* * *

A few days later Liam was released from the hospital. He looked very well. He was on loads of medication and had been told to take it easy. However, his interpretation of "taking it easy" had nothing to do with the drink, just the work. He said that they told him at the hospital that he had been working too hard and that he needed to rest.

True to his word, he did take it easy – so easy in fact that I hardly saw him for the next few weeks. After he helped stock up the bar in the mornings he would make some excuse that he had to go somewhere and I would not see him for the rest of the day. On these occasions he would meet up with some friends and go to a pub called The Clock House. I have no idea where it was; all I had been told about it was that they sold poteen, which could be lethal as it was about one hundred per cent pure spirit. This pub, I later discovered, mixed this poteen with ordinary whiskey. When Liam started drinking it there was no stopping him. He would come home in an awful state.

On one particular night John and myself were still working in the bar when Liam fell in the door. He was so pissed that John had to help me to get him up the stairs to bed. After about ten minutes or so we heard a big bang coming from upstairs. I thought that maybe Sarah had woken and thrown something out of her cot. When I ran up I saw Liam trying to get out of the landing window, which had a fifty-foot drop into the back yard. He thought that he could fly. I shouted for John to come up and help me, as Liam was far too strong for me to hold down on my own. It took us both a good ten minutes to calm him down, with John finally sitting on top of him. He was totally out of his mind.

* * *

Life seemed to be going from bad to worse. A few weeks later Liam was downstairs working the bar on his own and I was upstairs with Sarah, settling her to sleep, when I noticed that for some reason it had gone very quiet down in the bar. There was no music coming from the jukebox, which was unusual. I couldn't even hear the smack of a snooker ball. I headed down to see if everything was all right.

What I saw frightened the life out of me. All of my fears about retaliation from the IRA came flooding back to me. My husband was being held up against the wall by a man who had one hand around his throat and a gun to his head.

I knew who he was and I knew what he was as he was often in the bar with others. I also knew that the gang around him were all carrying guns. They had always done so and we had just let it go to prevent any trouble. Now I was confronted with this sight and I told myself that, whatever happened, I was not going to let these bastards think I was frightened of them, even though my knees were absolutely trembling, and the blood had gone cold in my body.

So I walked a few steps towards them, looked at the guy who was holding Liam, and I shouted, "What the bloody hell do you think you are doing? Put him down and put that bloody gun away, or else you're barred!"

After the words came out I thought to myself, *Jesus, what a stupid thing to say: "you're barred"*. I didn't think he was worried about being barred! But I think he was as shocked as I was at what I had said and that I had the balls to stand up to them. He instantly took the gun away from Liam's head and let go of his throat.

All the other punters were just standing around terrified, saying nothing. Not one bloody man among them, I thought. "What the hell is going on in here?" I yelled. Nobody spoke, so I turned to Liam and told him to get out of the bar and go upstairs. He went off like a dog with his tail between his legs.

I didn't know what to do next and no one would answer me so I just said, "Jesus, I need a drink."

As I walked nervously towards the bar I asked Mr Gunman if he would like one as well. He said, "Thanks, Ann. I'd love a whiskey." He continued, "Look, I'm sorry about that. Don't take it personally."

I said, "Ah, forget it. Sure I know that Liam could pick a fight with the devil himself."

I didn't know what else to say. I knew that I was treading on dangerous ground and I didn't want to antagonise the situation any further.

I made myself busy behind the bar as I didn't want anyone to see how shaken I was. My legs were like jelly and my hands were shaking so much that I was in danger of dropping glasses. All I really wanted to do was to throw everybody out and close up the pub so that I could get myself and my thoughts together.

Liam didn't come back down that night and when I went up to the bedroom later he was asleep. Not a bother on him. He didn't mention a thing about what happened the next day, not even to say sorry for putting me in such a dangerous situation. When I pushed him about what had caused the flare-up he refused to say – he just got up and walked off to his usual haunt, The Clock House.

* * *

After that incident and with the way Liam's drinking habits were going, I got very down and I no longer enjoyed running the pub. I was terrified that there would be another incident and was constantly wary of his mood swings and terrible temper. He was also starting fights with the customers all the time because he was always fuelled up on booze. I didn't know from one day to another how things were going to work out or what trouble was to come to my door.

A few weeks after the episode in the bar, on a night when we had cleaned up early and headed off to bed, there was an unmercifully loud bang on the pub door. Not knowing what was going on, we both went downstairs and Liam shouted out, "Who's there?"

A voice shouted back, "It's the police. Can you open the door?"

Liam opened the door and let the officer in, wondering what was happening. The policeman said, "We have had a tip-off that there is a bomb on your premises. I would advise you to have a good look around."

And with that he turned on his heels and walked off! Not a word about helping us to find it, or if we did find it what we were to do with it; not a care for the young child asleep upstairs. We stared at each other, wondering what the hell we were supposed to do. We had nowhere to run to and no one to turn to for help. We ran up and checked on the baby and then spent the next few hours looking for a bomb. We pulled everything apart, searched every nook and cranny and found nothing.

We were just going upstairs when the phone rang. Liam said "You'd better answer it – it might be the police."

But it wasn't. A voice on the end of the line said, "It's a false alarm this time, but it may not be the next time," and hung up.

We both just stood staring at each other. I asked Liam if he had done anything to annoy "them" (the IRA) and he said that nothing had happened other than the fact that we hadn't given them the room.

I knew all along that that was the reason for everything

that had happened – the fight with Liam, his constant drinking (not that he really needed an excuse, but it helped), and now this.

* * *

After this episode I got seriously ill. The stress and strain had taken a toll on my body. I went to get up one morning and found that I could not keep my balance. My head was thumping and the room was spinning round. The doctor was called and he told me that I needed complete bed rest for a few days as I was exhausted. I was very worried about the baby as I knew that Liam, as much as he loved her, would not take good care of her. I was not sure if the childminder would be able to keep her for a few extra days.

Thankfully John came to my rescue again. He said that he would get his mother in to help and that she could stay in the spare room and he would stay as well. He knew what Liam would do.

We didn't see my husband for the three days that I was in bed. On the fourth day he came in at around nine o'clock in the evening, walked into my bedroom and started shouting, "There's nothing wrong with you! Get your arse out of bed this minute and go downstairs and do some bloody work!" I tried to reason with him but the more I did the more aggressive he became.

In the end, just to keep the peace and calm him down, I dragged myself out of bed, got dressed and went downstairs. I sat on the bottom step for a minute but there was no sign of my husband. When I crept back up, he was lying flat out on the bed, snoring – the same bed that he had dragged me out of minutes earlier.

Things didn't improve at all between us but we carried on as usual. The pub was as busy as ever and I had the childminder looking after the baby during the day so I could help out in the bar. Liam, of course, was still going off doing his own thing and coming back out of his head on booze. I was stuck in a rut and could see no way out.

* * *

One Sunday afternoon when the pub was heaving, the childminder came dashing through the bar in an awful state. I ran over to see what was wrong with her. I had been stressed out over Liam and the IRA in the past but nothing was to prepare me for what she told me. She had lost my little girl. She said that she had spent the last hour looking for her and no one had seen her anywhere. My heart almost stopped there and then and I stood frozen to the ground. Sarah, my beautiful two-year-old daughter, missing. She said that she was in the arcade playing on the slot machines when she noticed that my little girl was gone. I dropped everything, called to John to get Liam and asked him to ring the police.

Liam and I ran to the arcade and searched everywhere. By this time a lot of people had joined us, as John had let them know what was happening. I was terrified that Sarah would make her way to the beach looking for me, as she knew that I took her there all the time. I could feel the fear rising inside me with every moment.

After about two hours of searching frantically all over town, we went back to the arcade again, just in case we missed something, as it was very crowded. God must have been looking after us because we found Sarah with a couple who said that they had seen her wandering around the place on her own and that they were trying to find her mum and dad.

Relief rushed through my body. Without even asking them any more questions, I just picked my daughter up, thanked the couple and walked back to the pub.

But I never went into the bar. Not that day, or ever again. This for me was the final straw.

Later that day, we found out from the police just how much the two brothers who owned the pub hated each other. We were shocked at the lengths they were going to in their efforts to get one over on the other. Unfortunately, and unbeknown to us, we were the victims in this family feud. And our little girl had not just wandered off and been found by the couple that day.

It turned out that Andy's brother Tim had planned to get us out of the pub right from the start. He was so intent on destroying our lives that he had organised for the couple to snatch our child from the childminder at the first opportunity. He knew that, after all I had been through, this would be the final frontier and I would want to leave immediately.

He was also the one who had made the hoax phone call to the police about the "bomb" in the bar; the one who had frightened the wits out of us and left me terrified for the safety of my child every single night going to bed.

We were told that there had been a big bust-up between the brothers when we arrived on the scene to take over the pub. Liam and I knew nothing of this as Andy had told us that he had sorted things out with his brother and that Tim was supposedly very happy for us to be there because he felt the pub was becoming a burden. But this couldn't have been further from the truth.

Tim and Andy had apparently never got on, but Andy had agreed to let his brother run the pub for six months, to get him started in a job. But in that time the business had gone downhill so rapidly that Andy was at risk of losing everything. He knew that he had no choice but to turf his brother out, blood or no blood. Therefore we became the scapegoats between the two siblings – and as far as Tim was concerned, it didn't matter what happened to us in the process.

He was always nice to us when he was in the pub and made out that everything was fine, but it seems that he got very frustrated when the bomb hoax failed to make us run with our pants around our ankles. Looking back on events, after the fact, it all made sense. When Tim was around in the bar an argument always seemed to start up for some reason or another and he was always in the thick of it. It seems he thought that we would get upset with fistfights happening nearly every night and that might make us jump ship. But, to his dismay, nothing seemed to be working. His plan was going down the drain and his last hope was the abduction of our little girl.

By the time we got back to the pub that day the two brothers had been lifted by the police and the officers met us at the bar and told us all about the plan. They said that they had also picked up the couple who were with our daughter when we found her. It turned out that the woman was Andy's and Tim's sister and the man was her husband. They hadn't planned on hurting her – they just wanted to hold onto her for a few hours in a bid to scare us into getting out of the town.

And of course it worked. We headed straight upstairs and packed as much as we could and left.

We decided not to press charges against any of them because as far as we were concerned we were lucky to still have our daughter untouched and alive. And we were lucky to be still alive ourselves.

* * *

We had nowhere of our own to go so we headed off to stay with Liam's parents about a hundred miles away. It was not the best of arrangements, but it would have to do for the moment. If nothing else it gave us space to think about what we were going to do next and a bit of time to sort out our lives. We really felt as if we had been used like idiots over the last few months and we had fallen for it all, hook, line and sinker.

I felt very low, as though we would never have anything in our lives to cherish and there was no light at the end of the tunnel.

I didn't know how Liam was feeling and I didn't care. He had got us into this situation and he could offer us no way out. He was so engrossed in his drink that our problems didn't even exist to him. I could never get him sober enough to talk sense and to decide what we were going to do next. His family weren't too worried either. They knew him for what he was and I felt that no matter what he did they would just let him get on with it.

I couldn't speak to anyone about my fears or about what had happened in the pub. I had found myself in the middle of something that I had no control over. I couldn't trust anyone, not even my own husband, because when he got pissed God knows what he said or did. It frightened me, yet I felt it was just another hurdle to get over. It was just another disaster brought upon us by my alcoholic husband.

CHAPTER NINE

Losing Ann

When we eventually got ourselves together we moved back to England and into a lovely house given to us by social services. It was our first real home as a family because I never counted the flat or the pub as "home". We were very lucky in that we were given everything we needed in a rented house and I felt a surge of optimism for the first time in years.

Liam was still drinking. In fact he very nearly wrecked everything for us on our very first night there. He had gone out for a drink, despite me begging him not to, and I spent the whole of that first night in my new house worrying sick about whether he was dead or alive. He finally turned up about ten o'clock the next morning telling me that he had been arrested for being drunk and disorderly and for urinating in the church grounds. He had appeared in court

ANN KENNY

that morning and had been released after being fined ten pounds.

This put a dampener on things for me but I swore to myself that I wouldn't let it get me down. I was trying to be positive now and in my mind this new start could be the beginning of a whole new life together as a family.

We had our ups and downs as usual but I tried to be as good a wife as I could. I cooked, I cleaned and, when he came in at night pissed out of his head on beer and spirits, I allowed him use me for sex. I had no other option. It was better to let him have his way than for him to be screaming abuse at me, wrecking the house and waking our little girl.

I dreaded hearing the key turn in the door because I never knew how he would be. He was in and out of jobs all the time and he couldn't seem to hold any of them down – but somehow we always got by.

I had always wanted another baby yet I was terrified of the idea too, not knowing if I would be able to cope financially and emotionally given the circumstances I was living in. But God made that decision for me and shortly after we moved into the house I found out that I was pregnant. We were both delighted and I made up my mind that I would try to get myself organised early for this baby's arrival because I never knew from one day to the next how our lives would change. It all depended on Liam and his split-second decisions.

I was very tired all the time throughout that pregnancy. I was looking after Sarah and losing sleep at night worrying where her father was and if he'd actually make it home in one piece. There was many a night that I imagined he was dead on the side of the road somewhere after a drunken night's bingeing.

The pregnancy itself seemed to be going fine. The baby appeared healthy on my hospital visits and although they weren't worried about anything in the hospital, I was still frightened that she or he would end up very ill, like Sarah had been. I think this worry took its toll on me as well because I was absolutely shattered. I tried to take an odd afternoon nap when Sarah had a sleep but that was easier said than done. Liam had a grand life. He went out every morning and came back late at night. He didn't have to worry about the house, the baby or anything else. But I got by.

Finally, in August 1977, our second daughter Emma was born, weighing a healthy seven pounds and four ounces. I was absolutely delighted when I came around from the caesarean to find her next to me in her cot, as I was expecting her to be in the ICU ward attached to all kinds of wires like her sister had been. But no, here she was, as bright as a button, and not a wire in sight.

I asked the nurse to place her in my arms, as I was unable to bend over to pick her up after the operation. It felt so good to hold her and it was only then that I realised what I had missed when our first child was born. An overwhelming feeling of guilt ran through me at the thought that I had missed the first three days of our firstborn's life.

* * *

Time passed. Months turned into years, and little changed in our lives.

When things got really tough financially, I started childminding in the house. I loved my job and although I had a very early start it suited me perfectly because it meant that I didn't have to leave the house and I didn't have to get a childminder for myself. I did everything by the book – I told social services about my plan and they put me on a childminding course, and that was it.

There were many arguments with Liam throughout these years. He felt that if I was working then he didn't have to give me as much, if any, money to keep the home. His drinking days had started to get longer again as well and I had to beg him some nights to come home to kiss the kids goodnight. But I carried on as usual and I tried to shelter the kids as much as I could from him on his bad days.

The sad thing was that, on his good days, Liam was the ideal dad. It was like living with a Jekyll and Hyde character. When he was sober, he was absolutely brilliant with his kids. When the babies arrived he seemed to calm down a lot. If I felt tired and he wasn't hung-over he would just tell me to go back asleep and he would do the night feed. He never complained about it.

I managed to keep my job for about nine years, during which time I gave birth to our son Paul, who arrived into the world in April 1980, weighing in at seven pounds fourteen ounces. His father was so proud to have a little boy and he idolised him. I was really happy with my children and I lived every single day for them. They were, and always will be, my life and the main reason I battled through my marriage for all those years. Words just cannot explain how much they mean to me. They have seen many bad things within their family life over the years and although I tried my best to hide most of it from their eyes, they weren't blind. However, they knew that, despite the problems Liam and I had, both of us adored them.

Things were going along well for me working from home until one day Liam came in fuelled with alcohol and screaming abuse. He called me every name under the sun, labelling me as a whore, a tramp and a prostitute. I hadn't a clue what he was talking about and his ranting and raving had me panicking. It turned out that some other drunken lout in the pub had told him that he saw a strange man going in and out of my house all the time. Putting two and two together, and making six, he assumed that I was having an affair. Where I was meant to find time for this affair didn't even come into it – in Liam's mind, I was having an affair and that was that.

I was mystified initially about who he was talking about until it dawned on me that it must have been the father of one of the children who Liam's "friend" had seen coming into the house. He was an African man and his wife would normally pick the kids up in the afternoons but sometimes he would arrive early, around 2.30, and just sit there waiting on her. He never spoke to me, he was very serious, and I was too intimidated to ask him to leave, so he would just sit there and read until she arrived. He didn't believe it was his duty to look after the children so he never did the mother a favour by taking the child home for her. So this was obviously the man I was supposedly having an affair with.

I slept on the couch that night. Liam stayed in the next day and told the man's wife that I was a slut and that I was sleeping with her husband. And he told every mother who called over the next few days to drop off their kids that I wasn't fit to mind my own kids, never mind anyone else's, and that I was having an affair with one of the children's fathers. I was mortified.

Needless to say this was just the start of my problems and the name-calling and slagging matches continued, despite all my denials. Eventually I had to tell all the mothers that I couldn't mind their children any more and once again I was left penniless, with no support from my children's father.

And so my days of childminding came to an end.

* * *

After a while I heard about a job that was going in a pub just up the road from the house. I went to see the landlord and he took me on.

Again, things went well for a while and I was getting back on my feet financially. Then one day, about six months after I started, Liam came in drunk and caused havoc. This time he accused me of having an affair with the landlord, calling me a slut and a whore in front of the whole place. This led to a big brawl in the pub and ended up with Liam being laid flat out on his back with a wallop from someone. I lost my job yet again.

When our son started school I tried to find more work but I was too afraid to go back into childminding or bar work for fear of what might happen when he found out. But I really needed to earn some money. Liam was very seldom in full-time work and when he was he would drink what he earned – and more if he could find it.

I called into the local supermarket one morning to get some groceries. As I was walking out I stopped to look at the notice board and I saw a card advertising for someone to do some cleaning work. I took the number down and thought I would give it a ring to see what exactly I would have to do.

This job led to more work and I ended up doing two cleaning jobs a day and was there for my children morning and evening. I told Liam what I was doing but I never told him where the jobs were. I did not want him turning up at the house drunk.

* * *

Over the next few years my life carried on much the same, with Liam's drinking getting increasingly worse and family life disappearing rapidly out the window. One day when I was out shopping I met two women whom I vaguely knew. They stopped to greet me and then one of them said, "Is your husband an alcoholic?"

In my nervousness and shock at the question I simply answered, "I don't think so."

"Well," she said, "he is always bloody drunk and carrying on in the pub, acting the arsehole, and looking for fights."

I didn't know what to say or do. I was totally stunned at the way she had just blurted this out. It made me feel sick and humiliated. I quickly said my farewells and left the two of them standing there staring at me, imagining them gossiping about me. I felt their eyes bore into my back as I made my way up along the street. I'm sure they must have been thinking, *Poor cow, having a husband like that.*

So that evening when Liam eventually got home I asked him out straight if he was an alcoholic. It was a stupid question, but I felt that if I said the word it might just make the penny drop with him and he would stop and think about what he was doing with his life. His reply was, "Don't be stupid, of course I'm not an alcoholic. Who put that rubbish into your head?"

I didn't dare tell him who had said it or what I was told about his behaviour in the pub. I knew he would only go back there and cause an argument. I also came to the conclusion that if he was an alcoholic, he would know it himself. It was always better for me to keep my mouth shut.

I put up with my existence as it was and lived with alcoholism for the twenty-three years of my married life. It was very hard trying to cope with the simple everyday things in life and it just seemed to get worse with each passing day, month and year.

I found it very hard to concentrate on the day-to-day issues, as there was so much going on in my head. I was always worrying about Liam – how drunk he was going to be, what kind of mood he would be in when he eventually fell through the door. My days were shaped by his mood swings.

I also worried non-stop about money, mainly the lack of it, hoping that I would have enough to pay bills, buy food and clothe the children. Living from day to day was a struggle. My three children were a constant worry to me because they were forced to live their young lives out watching their father being verbally, mentally and emotionally abusive towards their mother – although he never, ever laid a finger on them. But I do feel that they were mentally abused since the day they could walk and talk.

I started to write down my thoughts and feelings on pieces of paper as the pressure of living with alcoholism grew. Sometimes, before I even got out of bed in the morning, I would have the day mapped out in my head. I used to call it "Living in my Head". Some days I didn't know who I was, never mind what I was. I had to tell myself that I was in fact a wife, a mother and, most importantly, a woman called Ann.

I had lost Ann years ago. I no longer recognised the woman I saw in the mirror, or associated her with the person that she had become. In my head Ann did not exist anymore. In her place was a woman who lived on her nerves, could just about cope with life, and most of all feared the sound of the key in the door. This person was good at pretending that everything was all right to the outside world, while inside she was hurting so much with the pain and struggle of living with an alcoholic.

At first when I started to write, it was only to get those thoughts out of my head before they sent me insane. However, the more I wrote the more I realised that it helped me to release some of the pressure that was building up inside my head every day. At first I was very careful about what I put down on paper as I was too afraid to read my own fears and thoughts back to myself. But as time went on I got over this and began to have faith in my own ability to deal with things as they arose.

I started my first diary in January 1989. My children at that time were aged fourteen, twelve and eight. So far they had lived all of their young lives with a drunken, abusive father – a father who loved his children and loved the idea of being a father, but not the responsibility. In the same way, he loved the idea of being a husband and having a wife, without having a clue what the word "marriage" actually meant.

One diary led to another and then another and to this day I still write down how I feel and think about things. Sometimes I find it's good to look back on them. It shows me where I have been and where I am now. It helps me put things into perspective. None of my children have ever read my diaries and publishing some of the more difficult parts is quite hard for me. But I know the value of writing my thoughts down because I am now strong enough to be able to cope with the heartache of re-reading them. As the wife of an alcoholic, as an abused child who had no one to love her and as a woman called Ann, who has fought through thick and thin and came out at the other end smiling, I am now strong enough to open my heart and my mind to others and to say, no matter how bad things are in your life – there is always hope.

CHAPTER TEN

Lost

When you live with an alcoholic, no two days are the same. In fact, some days, no two hours are the same. You dread waking up in the mornings because you know what the day has to bring with it and you dread going to bed at night because most of the time "the drunk" isn't in from the pub and you lie there panicking, wondering if he or she is dead or alive. Sometimes you might even wish that he would never come back.

It's a horrible existence. And that's all it is: an existence. You live your life from one moment to the next. You can't plan anything because you know the likelihood is that it will never happen anyway. You can't invite friends or family over because you know the night could end up a disaster if the drinking got out of hand. My children were and always will be my biggest concern and as a mother I tried to protect them as much as I possibly could from anything that could harm them, physically or mentally. As a mother it was my job to make sure that no matter what happened between their father and I, they would know and hear as little as possible. It was also my most difficult job. As the children got older it grew harder to protect them from the inevitable.

Every day was the same and Christmas Day was no different. Christmas of 1988 was one example. The kids had woken up early to see what Santa had left for them and their daddy had gone off to the pub for a Christmas drink. I busied myself in the kitchen, leaving the children to play with their new toys. We were all dying for the big Christmas dinner, the usual turkey and ham and roast potatoes. The kids were all excited. The table had been set and everything was ready to go. Except, of course, Liam.

We waited for hours for him to come home, everyone watching the door. He eventually staggered in the door, with the much-needed help of a couple of friends, at about five o'clock. He couldn't even stand, never mind speak. The children saw him come in but they carried on playing as if nothing was wrong. Sure, it was just the norm, really, only today was Christmas Day, a day for the children. But for Liam, it was like any other day; once the pub was open he was in it.

To keep the peace I reluctantly said that we would wait on daddy to have a sleep and we'd eat a bit later. I did this simply because I knew that if we ate without him there would be hell to pay. We were all starving, but the fear of his wrath would not allow us to start without him at the top of the table. We had to sit and wait until the drunk in the bed was in a fit state to join us. When we eventually all sat down on Christmas Day at around eight o'clock, we were all nervous wrecks as we sat there wondering if he would suddenly explode and ruin everything.

We never did anything unusual at Christmas, simply because we couldn't. Liam did his own thing anyway and it was always up to me to make sure as best I could that, if nothing else, at least the children were happy. We got through Christmas and St Stephen's Day by the skin of our teeth. We watched Liam come in night after night staggering around the place as he tried to find his bed. And as the days and weeks went on things just seemed to get steadily worse. Each year, I hoped and prayed that he would make a New Year's resolution and give up the drink, but I knew in my heart that it would have taken a blessed miracle for that to happen.

One particular day over that Christmas holidays he went out early and didn't come back until the next morning. It turned out that he had been in his sister's house all night drinking and he fell in the door absolutely pissed. It was ten o'clock in the morning and he was standing there demanding money off me for more drink. To keep him from shouting and roaring I gave him ten pounds.

"That's not enough," he shouted. "I need more."

"No! I don't have that kind of money to give to you to piss away."

With that he marched across to the front door, locked it and put the keys in his pocket. I knew that he was going to hurt me, so I picked up a big hairbrush from the table beside me and I threw it at him full force. I aimed at his face but he put his hands up to protect himself so it hit him in the face and hands. I ran to grab the spare keys from the shelf and raced out the door before he could come after me. I knew that I'd had a lucky escape that day and I thanked God that the kids weren't there to see what could have happened.

* * *

It's amazing how the lives of alcoholics go – because a couple of days later, when he was sober, I talked to him about how bad things were getting and how his drinking had to stop. I told him how terrified I was of his behaviour when he was fuelled up. I knew that when Liam was sober, and he realised how bad he had been the night before, he always felt guilty, and this time I think it really hit home.

He agreed that he had to do something about it. Not only was it causing so much trouble in the house but he was also broke. Every penny he had was spent on alcohol and not having any money in his pocket was getting to him. So in January I went with him to the alcoholic unit at our local hospital. There they breath-tested him. He had an alcohol level of 195 – which is very high, especially for the morning after the night before. I nearly hit the floor when they said that they couldn't do anything for him until the alcoholic level was reduced. We would have to come back later that evening to have it monitored again. Thankfully Liam didn't head off to the pub as he would normally do; he didn't run away and drown his sorrows. We went back that night to the clinic and the level had gone down a bit. He was, however, in a very bad way at this stage, shaking from the lack of booze in his system. The doctor put him on tablets that he said would help with the withdrawal symptoms of the drink and calm down the shakes. Then – I couldn't believe what I was hearing – they told him to go home. They sent him off, just like that, and I had an awful night with him screaming and shouting and being very aggressive.

Two days later they had no choice but to admit him as his condition was getting continually worse as the hours of sobriety dragged on. He didn't look well at all. He was transferred over to the main hospital for a check-up. The doctor asked him what had happened to his hand, as it was very bruised. Liam told him that he had banged it off something. I piped up, "No you didn't. I threw the hairbrush at him as he wouldn't let me out of the house." He was mortified but I had decided that week that I wasn't going to cover up for him anymore.

They kept him in for just two days to start his detox and when he got out he looked so much better. It had been a week since he'd had a drink and I prayed that he would continue to stay sober.

He did well to begin with. We had the usual worries about falling off the wagon. When a good friend of his died suddenly just a few weeks later, I was terrified that, once the funeral was over and everyone headed back to the pub, he would automatically order a drink, but thank God he didn't. However, it didn't last long.

St Patrick's Day came along. Traditionally, this is a time when all of the Irish in London meet up in their locals for a few pints to celebrate Ireland's national feast day. I was sick worrying how he would deal with this and my heart sank when he headed off to the pub saying that he would be fine and he'd only have one or two.

An alcoholic can never have "just one" drink; the addiction is so strong that it's nearly impossible to stop once you start. He had lasted a whole eight weeks since he'd had a tipple and then he went and ruined it all again. He only had two drinks that day but there began the merry-go-round. All of the hard work of the previous few weeks was just flushed down the toilet. We ended up having a huge argument in the car park of the local supermarket that day because I felt so let down and so annoyed at him for being so selfish.

By the end of May he was back in hospital again because his drinking had got so bad. His mood swings were dreadful. Some days he was up and some he was down and I had to prepare myself every day for dealing with whatever I met when I arrived at his bedside. He stayed in hospital for nearly two weeks going through all sorts of mood swings, but bit by bit he improved again and when he eventually came home he was a different man and the kids were delighted to see their daddy back, all happy and loving to them. But his transformation this time lasted a whole five days – and then it was back to normal with the same old speech: "I can handle it."

He did go to a counsellor, but he went in for most of his visits half-pissed. I would see the annoyance on the face of the counsellor and think to myself, *Imagine what it's like for me having to deal with this crap every single day.*

* * *

That summer, we decided to go back to Ireland for a holiday. But we missed the ferry from Holyhead because Liam was sleeping off a hangover and I couldn't wake him. We got to the port late and I spent the day walking around Holyhead with the kids on my own while their father got pissed in the local pubs. We eventually managed to make it back to Ireland for our family holiday and he spent the entire time knocking back pints in his old haunts. I thought to myself, *Why do we even bother coming here when he just does exactly the same thing in Ireland as he does in London?* The only good thing about going away was that the kids got to see their cousins and enjoy the open air of the countryside.

We missed the boat going home for the same reason as we missed it going over. His hangovers messed us up again. We left Dublin a day late on the morning of the 2nd of September. Little did I know at the time that this day was to be one of the worst days of my life.

As we drove along the M1 motorway Liam took a fit or a blackout at the wheel of the car, doing seventy miles per hour in the middle lane. The fit, we later found out, was caused by all the drinking he had done back in his hometown. We were only saved from being killed by my quick reaction and the will of God. The three kids were in the back of the car and I was in the passenger seat. I managed to shove Liam out of the way when he collapsed and pulled the wheel as hard as I could, swerving across two lanes and into a ditch.

When they say that your whole life flashes in front of you at times like this, believe me, it's true. My first thoughts were for my children and we were blessed that none of us was killed that day. We were all taken to hospital with minor injuries.

Liam had caused this accident because he was drunk behind the wheel of our car. He never once thought about the safety of his family when he turned the key in the ignition to take us home. He also never once apologised for his actions; he never seemed to show, or have, any remorse for what he did. I was sickened by his attitude when he simply said that we should all just be thankful that we were not killed. I remember thinking, *How could he be so thoughtless?* His children could have been killed that day, their lives taken from them by their ignorant, selfish father. If that had happened I would have had no hesitation in throwing him in front of a car, a bus or a train. In the days that followed I felt nothing but hatred for my husband. I wished so much that God would have taken him away from us all.

* * *

A few days after we got home Liam was due back in hospital for some blood tests. We weren't talking and he was still drinking. But he wasn't prepared for being told that day that he had sclerosis of the liver. He was warned by the specialist to give up alcohol completely or risk dying very young. Of course, true to form, he totally ignored the advice of the doctor; when he left the hospital he went straight to the pub. At that stage I felt I had no choice but to give up. The only person who could help Liam was Liam and he didn't seem to give a damn.

I tried to put the doctor's warning to the back of my head and went to my local church to thank God for saving all of our lives on the M1. I asked the parish priest if there were some penance that I should do, as I felt that God had given me a second chance in life and I wanted to repay him. He told me that I was doing enough penance living with an alcoholic.

I also went to see my doctor that same day as I was feeling very depressed. He told me that I was suffering from delayed shock. He suggested that Al-Anon might be good for me.

I was so naive that I thought this was a tablet that he was giving me and I asked, "Is it on prescription?"

He laughed and explained, "No Ann, Al-Anon is a self-help group for the families of alcoholics." He told me where and when they met and I agreed that I would give it a go.

I went to my first meeting on the 13th of September. Liam agreed to come to the venue with me and go into an AA meeting, just to see what it was all about. The Al-Anon meetings, it turned out, were only for the families of alcoholics, not for the abusers themselves. That's why Liam went to the AA meeting. When he agreed to go, my first thought was, *Big deal – if it wasn't for his selfishness we wouldn't be here in the first place*. But I held my tongue.

I found that first meeting pretty daunting. I was going to try to get myself sorted out, as I couldn't stand the arguments at home anymore. But as I sat there I asked myself, *Why am I here? I It's not me with the problem – it's bloody well him!* But I sat there and I listened as people, who remained anonymous, told their stories – each one similar to the other . . . similar to my own. I didn't know how I felt that night, but they told me as I left that I would need to go to at least six meetings to judge if Al-Anon was right for me. I agreed to come back again sometime but I wasn't sure when that would be. Liam didn't talk much about his meeting but I don't think it had any effect on him because he didn't bother going back again.

Over the next few weeks we went back and forth to the hospital. Liam's mood swings were a nightmare. He continued to meet up with his counsellor and some days I would go in as well, but I was really annoyed at the way in which I, the partner of the alcoholic, was just ignored at these meetings. All the bullshit that Liam was filling him with was taken as gospel without even consulting me, the other person in this horrible nightmare. At one stage I had to sit for an hour listening to my half-pissed husband telling this man a pack of lies about how he hadn't had a drink and how he was trying his very best to stay sober.

When Liam got up to go to the toilet I took the opportunity to tell the counsellor that he was talking a load of rubbish. He told me that he believed Liam and that I should have more faith in him. He said that I should support him more, instead of always giving out to him. I was sick. I felt like asking him if he was wearing rose-tinted glasses; how could he not see that Liam was sitting there drunk? Instead I told him to look out of the window at the pub across the road and to make sure that he looked out again when we left because that's exactly where Liam would be heading. I'll never know if he did look out that window, but Liam didn't let me down.

His drinking continued to occupy our whole existence. Our whole lives seemed to be put on stand-by, as we were never sure of the way he would behave when he got home. I was always on the look-out for his temper or if something was not to his liking. *Christ*, I thought, *what a way to live*.

He would accuse me of stealing money from him or not looking after him properly and then he would pack up and go to his sister's house. The only problem was, he always came back. There was a time in the late 1980s when I thought that I would much prefer if God were to take me than for me to continue with my life as it was. At times I felt very low, even suicidal, and the only think that kept me from taking an overdose was the thought of the damage I would do to my three children. They were the innocent victims caught up in the middle of all this chaos through no fault of their own. However, when I was at my lowest, I thought my body would not be able to take any more stress. Things were getting worse by the day and he was drinking more than ever before. We were arguing non-stop. The pressure I felt on my brain was so bad that I thought I could just collapse at any moment.

It was always easier for me to put my thoughts into poetry and so I wrote this one, trying to get all of my frustration out.

LOST

I feel my brain is slowly bleeding
With all this crying, and all this weeping
I feel so lost, I feel so low
I wonder if it's time to go?
Go where? I do not know,
Or should I stay and make a stand?
And leave the rest in God's safe hands.

However, I had the kids to think about and I couldn't just be selfish like Liam and do whatever I wanted. I had to be there for my children, no matter what. They only really had one parent and that was me; so it was my duty to protect them as much as I could. The children had been very good through everything but I knew only too well that secretly they were having a hard time. Sarah had been plagued with asthma and her breathing seemed to get worse and worse day after day – all caused by stress. Paul was wetting the bed and Emma never realised that I could hear her crying in her sleep at night. It was so unfair that they had to go through all of this.

In May 1990 Liam was fined £100, a lot of money back then, and was given two hundred hours' community service, for drinking and driving while he was banned from being behind the wheel. Yet again he never stopped to think about the rest of us and how handing out £100 for his selfish act would affect his wife and children.

His weight had started to go down rapidly by now. He had of course ignored the hospital's warnings that he would die if he carried on drinking. For him, nothing changed.

Liam and I had no intimacy in our relationship at this stage. We never had sex and I never wanted to with him. But I felt very alone at times, struggling through with a brave face and a sad heart. I slept in my son's bedroom in the top bunk most of the time, simply because I couldn't abide the smell of drink from Liam's breath. He would also be ranting and raving and tossing and turning all the time. On the nights when we did sleep in the same bed I would either end up on the edge of the bed or sleeping on the floor.

* * *

Our marriage was well and truly over and in April of 1992 I rang a solicitor to enquire about a separation as I felt that it was the only thing left for me to do. There was nothing more in my marriage worth saving; the good had gone from it many years ago. I told my eldest daughter and thankfully she stood by me. Even Liam's sister agreed with me, saying that I was a martyr to have lasted so long.

The solicitor gave me all the details and I said I would get back to him. I took all the paperwork home and told Liam what I intended doing. Of course, he showed no interest whatsoever. The solicitor had advised me that I should ask Liam to leave. But that was easier said than done. I was afraid of Liam's reaction if I even suggested that he leave, but after hearing the solicitor say it was the only way forward I knew I had no choice but to try. At first he went berserk at the suggestion, telling me that it was his home as much as it was mine, which of course was true, but after many weeks of screaming and shouting at each other, I think he realised there was no going back and he eventually moved out into his own flat. Needless to say the harassment continued. He would regularly call around to the house in a drunken stupor, screaming and shouting and upsetting the children. But we all just learned to ignore him and tried to get on with our lives as best we could.

Many a time I thought how different it could all have been if he had only stopped drinking altogether. You read in the papers every day about young people dying for no reason, people who should have had their whole lives ahead of them. Then there was Liam, slowly drinking himself to death of his own choice. He had started to have more blackouts than ever before and this was not a good sign. I could not go anywhere without him being there. I felt like he was a leech or a cancer that was eating away at me until I either gave in or slowly lost my strength and all respect for myself.

Every day began with a row, mainly over money. It was so disheartening. One day he beat me up after he claimed that I owed him £20 I knew nothing about. I was a nervous wreck. There were times when I felt like putting a knife through his chest. I found it hard to believe at times that he could be such a wicked, deceiving, cunning, lying, horrible bastard.

At one stage he even started to follow me when I left the house. I had told him to leave us and not come back and so, to make sure he didn't lose control over me, he would follow me and then start shouting abuse at me in the streets. One day the kids actually called the police to take him away after he came to the house drunk and started to wreck the place.

That was how bad he had become. I didn't press charges but it gave him a fright at least.

Another time I seriously contemplated locking Liam in our son's bedroom, thinking I could buy him a bottle of cheap whiskey every day and let him get on with it, until he either had enough or he killed himself. The only thing that stopped me was the knowledge that with my luck I would probably run out of money first.

* * *

I started going back to the Al-Anon meetings. I had been there a few years earlier when the doctor first advised me to go, but at that time I could not get my head around the programme that they followed. I just wasn't in the right place or the right frame of mind to accept what was on offer. But this time I went back because, just like an alcoholic, I had reached my rock bottom. This time I felt that I was ready to listen and to accept that I wasn't the only one going through this living hell. Sometimes I felt they were a great help and at other times I just sat there, unable to speak. But all in all I found the meetings very helpful. They kept me sane.

You just have to sit there and listen because the whole idea of the meeting is to be non-judgemental about anyone. I realised quickly that when I had first attended Al-Anon, my heart just hadn't been in it. I asked myself at the time, *Why am I sitting around a table and getting no feedback?* But I later found out that the whole idea of Al-Anon is to be able to sit there with like-minded people and talk about your problems, knowing that no-one in that room will judge you. They told us that talking about your problems helped you to find your answers, but I had been writing about them for years and I still hadn't found the answers.

One night they spoke a lot about motives. I thought, *What are motives anyway? Are they something we do without thinking or do we have to think about it before we do it?* It was all too confusing back then for me.

It really annoyed me how little support there was in the 1980s and 1990s, and right up to today, for the families of alcoholics. If it wasn't for Al-Anon there would be nothing. If you are unlucky enough to have no support from friends or family and you feel that no one could understand what you are going through unless they have been there themselves, then Al-Anon can be a lifesaver. At times it can be an absolute nightmare just trying to get through each day with no help whatsoever. Back then for me it was so frustrating. There was many a time when I brought Liam to hospital because he was uncontrollably sick and they just sent us back out the door because he was pissed. He went in and out of rehab on dozens of occasions and every time he came out we thought, *This could be it – the new Liam.*

I think the longest period of sobriety he ever had lasted for about eight months. It was a really lovely time for us all. Liam looked and felt happy, and we were happy. However, no matter how good it seemed, we always felt as if we were walking on eggshells, waiting for the bubble to burst, and so afraid of saying anything that could possibly trigger him off on a drinking spree again. But on most occasions when he came out of rehab, within a matter of days, not even weeks, it was back to the same thing all over again.

It was so embarrassing when I would meet someone one day and say, "He is doing great", and then two days later to have to say, "Actually, he's in a bad way again." I was always mortified when people asked me how "the other half" was keeping. It was like they knew anyway but just felt obliged to ask because they felt sorry for me. My life was just one big embarrassment.

* * *

One of the most humiliating times in my life was when I became a prisoner's wife. I never thought I would see the day when I would be walking inside a prison gate to visit a relative. But nothing is ever certain in this life. No one knows what each day will bring.

It all began when Liam was caught drunk at the wheel of the car at ten o'clock on a Sunday morning – after he had crashed into another car at a set of traffic lights. My husband, who always bragged about how clever he was, had tried in his drunken stupor to get away from the scene only to crash into more cars further down the road. While other drivers managed to swerve to get out of his way, one driver was not so lucky and crashed into the central reservation, causing damage to their car as well as to themselves. Liam was eventually arrested.

I knew nothing of this until about five o'clock in the evening, when two police officers turned up at my door to tell me that he had been taken into custody for dangerous driving. My first reaction was that it served him bloody right, as he would never listen to my warnings of the dangers of drink driving.

When he was released he didn't even have the guts to phone me and tell me himself – instead, he got his niece to do it for him. She told me that he was thinking of running away to Ireland as his solicitor had told him that he was almost certainly facing a prison sentence. He never once thought about how his family would feel about all of this; he was running away from his problems once again. He was gutless and selfish.

Liam was badly beaten up by the police while he was in custody. I could not believe the state of his body where they had trounced him. He had terrible bruises all down his side when I visited him. I asked him if he had been hurt when he crashed. He said no, but he had put up a good fight when they tried to arrest him. Of course, Liam being Liam, he was also very mouthy to the police. In his defence, though, the bruises were so bad that I took photos of all the marks in case he ever needed them to prove that he had been assaulted either in custody or whilst being arrested. He never did get a chance to take it any further though. I am not sure if there would have been much point, considering his crime.

He eventually went to court and was given a jail sentence. I was absolutely mortified to have to sit in a courtroom and listen to the full story of how my drunken husband had stupidly got into a car that night and caused mayhem. I sat numb in the seat, as he was sentenced to fifteen months behind bars and led away. Thankfully Sarah was there to help me out of the courtroom.

I didn't know whom I felt sorrier for, Liam or me. He did bring it all on himself and he did need to pay the price for all the trouble he had caused; but it was still very hard as his wife to be left on my own when I walked out of the courtroom. I had no one to tell me what was happening or to comfort me.

Liam was sent to Belmarsh and we were left to pick the pieces up and carry on as we always had done. Nobody seemed to care what happened to us. We didn't do anything but we were made to feel as if we had. I wrote a poem later about how I felt that day.

> I sat in the courtroom, trying hard not to cry
> When all of my insides just wanted to die
> I sat and I listened to what they were saying
> My hands held tight, in my mind I was praying
> I sat and I heard of what you did that day
> And the mayhem you caused in
> Trying to get away.

* * *

While Liam was in prison I got my solace from the Al-Anon meetings. I really got into the programme; I found that it gave me back my confidence and the strength to be able to cope with life at that very difficult time. At a meeting one night someone said that not everyone finds sobriety; this I now truly believe. Unfortunately, I thought that night, I happened to be married to one of those few who will never give up alcohol. That particular night was very hard for me because the reality suddenly dawned that Liam was in fact a hopeless case. I was filled with despair.

He was released early from prison in November and immediately started to drink. And so the cycle began again. He was back in rehab six weeks after coming out of prison, and we spent Christmas and the New Year, as usual, trying to pretend that everything was alright.

Six months after he was released from prison I could see how his body was giving up the ghost and I forced him to go to the doctor; who sent him for more tests to our local main hospital. The results came back showing that Liam had lost eighty per cent of his liver, but as the doctor said, the liver is a great organ that can recover itself. He was also jaundiced. He was admitted there and then and I left the hospital relieved that someone was finally listening to me.

The next day when I called to the ward I met the doctor again. He pulled me to one side and said, "Remember, Ann, what I told you yesterday – that Liam has lost eighty per cent of his liver? Well, I'm afraid the news is a lot worse, Ann; he hasn't lost eighty per cent – he has lost it all."

At that time I think my mind shut down. I just said "thank you" and walked out of the hospital. I didn't even go back in to talk to Liam; I just wanted to escape. I could not imagine how he could have coped so long with absolutely *no* liver function.

Just days later, I was told that he had two weeks to live. I was devastated. I could not take in what they had said; my mind could not accept it. I stared into space with my heart beating so fast I was sure that the doctor could hear it.

My first thought was, *How am I going to tell the children?* I sat in a tiny room on my own trying to make sense of things and the only prayer that came into my mind was the

Serenity Prayer that we say in Al-Anon. I repeated it over and over again.

> God, grant me the Serenity to accept the things I cannot change,
> Courage to change the things I can,
> And the Wisdom to know the difference.

I was so grateful at that time for Al-Anon because I knew that the meetings were all that were getting me through from day to day. I would need them now more than ever.

When I broke the news to the children later that day they were, as expected, devastated. No matter what had happened throughout the years, Liam was their father and my husband. I had gone through hell and back and wished him dead on so many occasions and yet now, knowing that he was finally leaving us, I felt numb.

One day I headed into the hospital early. Liam looked terrible. His sister helped me to clean and change him and make him as comfortable as we could as he lay in the bed. He was on morphine at this stage to ease the pain. While his sister had gone to get some coffee for us I sat beside him holding his hand and I broke down and cried. Suddenly I felt a hand on my head. Liam had woken up. He looked at me and said, "Don't cry, Ann, I love you very much." Before I could answer him he had drifted off to sleep again.

* * *

My husband, my first love, who had fought this awful addiction called alcoholism for most of his adult life, finally lost his battle and died one night in the summer of 1997 at the age of forty-six. He left this world at 1.50 am. He had chosen the life he had and unfortunately he had also chosen not to change it. If he had, maybe things would have been completely different for us all as a family. The one thing we were all thankful for was the fact that he was now finally out of pain and hopefully at peace with himself. He died in my arms and as I laid him back in the bed I stood at the foot of it.

I suddenly felt as if someone was wrapping a blanket around me and saying, "You have done all you can. Now we will look after you. Liam will be looked after on the other side." I have no idea to this day who or what said it, but the peace and the calm that came over me at that moment was a blessing, as it allowed me to cope.

Before Liam died they told me in the hospital that they would not consider him for a liver transplant. I had never even asked them to consider it as I didn't think that it was possible. But why even tell me something like that – why put the thought into my head when they knew it was too late? I was very annoyed because I had cried for help so often at the beginning, long before he became seriously ill, and yet no one listened, no one seemed to care.

IT'S NOT YOUR PROBLEM

"It's not your problem."
How many times have I heard that before?
From doctors and nurses and many, many more.
"It's not your problem, you do not drink."
But my mind is confused and I cannot think.
Why don't you listen and hear what I say
As I live with the problem every night and day?
"Your partner must ask if he wants to be helped."
But I keep telling you, he's too ill to ask himself.
Who do I turn to? Who do I see?
Who do I talk to that will listen to me?
The tension I'm feeling is bursting my brain.
I'm so scared and I'm frightened.
Am I going insane?
He's dying so slowly in front of my eyes
But I can't do a thing because they don't realise
He's too ill to ask for the help that he needs
So the problem again just falls back on me.
It's too late, doctor. He died yesterday.
When I asked for your help you just turned me away.
"It was not your problem. It was the disease that he had."
Tell that to my children as they bury their Dad.

* * *

Time seemed to stand still for a while after Liam died. Some days we half expected him to walk stumbling through the door, pissed as usual. I have to admit that I didn't miss the drink or the smell of it as I entered my home, nor did I miss the fear and tension that went with it.

I had good days and bad nights for a long time after he passed. Many a night I'd end up crying myself to sleep. At times I thought that I was coping well with his death, then out of the blue I'd get an aching feeling deep inside of me which hurt like hell. Sometimes the pain and the loneliness were unbearable. For many months after his death I found it hard to accept that he was gone. I would say to myself that he was "just somewhere". I couldn't pray for him, because then I would have had to accept that he was dead.

My children coped with their father's death in their own individual ways, and as best they could, but there were no words that I could say to them that would have helped ease their pain. However, I am grateful for one thing – as a family we grew closer after Liam passed away and this I feel helped us heal quicker.

It took us a long time to accept that we could finally, and without guilt, live our lives the way we wanted to. Up until then we didn't know what a "normal" life was, what "normal" people did, as we were just used to living with an alcoholic, and to us that was "normal". Now gone was the worry, the fear and the tension of trying to cope with alcoholism. Our lives, albeit devoid of a husband and dad, were only about to begin.

CHAPTER ELEVEN

Going Back to My Roots

When I was sixteen and first discovered that I was not Rossie Nolan but Anastasia O'Brien, I was totally dumbfounded. It was very hard for me to take it all in. I was very young and very naïve. My foster mother had told me to take no notice of what it said on my birth certificate. I went along with it, of course, because I genuinely didn't know what else to do. I kept it all bottled up inside me waiting for the day when I would be old enough to know what to do.

But I loved the name Anastasia as it sounded so grand. I often wondered why my birth mother had given me such a lovely name and where she had heard it. Was it her own name? Had she called me after herself because she felt so bad having to give me away to strangers? When I said the name Anastasia I would let my mind drift, imagining that I had been born into a wealthy, sophisticated, respected family. I often thought about my birth mother. Who was she? Where did she live? Was she rich? Did she live in a big house?

They say that most people who have been fostered or adopted will at some time or other try to find out who their birth mother was and possibly their birth father. It's a natural instinct, a curiosity, I suppose, as we always feel that there is a void in our lives that we need to fill. I used to call my life a big jigsaw with lots of missing pieces that would some day be filled in.

As the years went by I became more eager to fill in the pieces of the puzzle, to find out who I really was. But I let so many things get in the way of my search – and it somehow never seemed to be the right time. There were many times throughout my turbulent marriage when I longed to break free and go in search of "me". But I could never bring myself to leave Liam. I would have felt too guilty leaving him to cope alone. It was always the way with me – I put other people's needs before my own.

There was many a time during my marriage when I dreamed of searching for my roots, but I knew I could not have gone through with it while I was still married to Liam. I would never have had the time to start searching, because I never really had any free time to myself. My whole world back then revolved around Liam. I never knew from one day to another how he would be – whether he'd come home sober or fall in the door. Just hearing the sound of his key in the door would turn my stomach inside out for fear of what may lie ahead. So I lived from one hour to the next in the hope that things might change and that *something* would make him realise that the drinking had to stop. Through it all I concentrated on my children, on giving them the best life I could give them in the circumstances. For years I felt that it would be better to stay with him to give the children a father figure. I only wished that this father figure could have been one they could have looked up to, be proud of, brag to their friends about, but I realised after some time that not all families are perfect and we weren't the only ones in the world with problems.

There were many times over the years when I bore the brunt of Liam's aggression and frustration. And each morning I woke in the bed beside him I prayed that this would be the day when it would all change, that God would work one of his miracles and make him see sense. It was of course all pie in the sky, but it kept me going, living in hope. My mind was too occupied with what was happening in my own home to even contemplate trying to find out what had happened thirty or forty years before when I had been abandoned. And so I put all thoughts of tracing my roots to the back of my mind for many years.

However, Liam's death in 1997 made me stop and think. It suddenly dawned on me in a big way that my children knew everything about their father, his parents (their grandparents), their aunts, uncles, cousins and so on, and how little they knew about me and my side of the family. It struck me that if I died they would know little or nothing about me. They would always know me as their mum but they would never know who Anastasia O'Brien was. So I made up my mind to begin the search for my roots.

* * *

I had started to see a counsellor after Liam died to get my head together. I had been working a lot with Al-Anon and attending the meetings helped to keep me sane because I got to meet like-minded people who had spent their lives living with an alcoholic. They knew only too well how hard it was to cope every single day, never mind every week.

But I knew that there were issues affecting me that had nothing to do with Liam and his problems and so I started to attend a counsellor called Sally and with her help and encouragement a lot of the things I had kept buried inside me for years were finally brought to the surface.

I attended Sally quite regularly and over time I opened up a lot and revealed things that I never thought I could even think about, never mind talk about again. We spoke about the life I had lived at the hands of my foster parents – the beatings, the abuse, both mental and physical, and the sheer sense of feeling unloved. Slowly but surely I revealed the tragedy of my childhood and she helped me through every step of the way.

But of course, like most abused people, there were things that I held back. I don't know if I did it purposely or subconsciously, but I did it. One of those things related to my grandfather. I had kept it all in the back of my mind until one night it all came back to me with a bang and the reality of it left me shattered.

I had taken a lift from a friend of mine called Martina. As we drove along she said, "I think I'm coming down with the 'flu."

"You should try putting some whiskey into your tea," I advised, remembering as I spoke that I used to have that myself as a child when I was very young.

"Where did you hear of that cure?" Martina asked me.

"I used to be given it as a little girl," I said. "I always slept well at night after a big mug of whiskey and tea."

She sat back in the seat looking very surprised. "Who would give a child that, for God's sake?"

I said, "My grandfather did when I had to sleep in his bed."

She looked at me with shock written all over her face and said, "You would never give a child whiskey, Ann – it would kill them. Why was it given to you?"

I told her that they, meaning my mother and grandfather, always gave it to me when I had to sleep with my granddad. It was only as the words came out of my mouth that I realised what I had said. I had never mentioned this to anyone before. Sleeping with grandfather was something I had always kept to myself.

Having spoken the words, like a bolt of lightning all those years of secret cuddles and touches and sleeping beside him in his old bed came flooding back to me, and I felt physically sick.

"I have to go," I told Martina, flinging the door open and dashing from the car. The memories were racing through my head and I felt weak.

As I was getting out of the car I heard Martina call after me, "Ann, can I say something? You need to speak about this – if not to me then to someone else. Are you still seeing Sally?"

"Yes."

"Well, promise me you'll tell her what you just told me next time you see her."

"I will," I said.

When I got indoors I headed straight for the bathroom as I felt I was going to throw up. But nothing came out. I felt nauseous and light-headed and I sat on the floor and cried until I could cry no more. I tried to put the thoughts of being in that bed out of my mind; I couldn't handle all those feelings all on my own.

That evening I headed off to an Al-Anon meeting. I felt that it was the best thing to do instead of being stuck in the house alone, dwelling on everything. My son, who was still living with me, was out for the night, so I thought if I were with other people it would take my mind off things.

* * *

I kept my appointment with Sally, who at this time I was seeing every fortnight. She was keeping me strong. I was delighted that I was still seeing her when all of this came to the fore, because I don't think I could have coped if she hadn't been there for me to fall back on. I felt that she was the only person I could trust and she always led me in the right direction when I needed someone to tell me what to do next. So when we met up a few days later I told her about the conversation I'd had with Martina in the car. I told her about the nights when I would be given this "drink" to make me sleep when I was a child. I told her how I used to hurt for days afterwards.

As the memories came flooding back again, I told Sally of the nights when I would sleep with grandfather and then wake up in agony the next morning. I always thought that they must have beaten me during the night for some reason, yet I could never figure out what it was that I had done wrong. It's horrible to think that my very first thought on waking every morning as a child in that house was whether or not they would beat me for something that day. Imagine, as a little girl, having to think like that as soon as you opened your eyes each morning!

I told Sally that it was my mother who would bring in the tea. I felt that she knew all along what was happening. He would reach into the back of the wardrobe, take out the bottle of whiskey and pour it into my mug, telling me to drink up. Sometimes I would gag on the taste and the smell of it but he would hold the mug to my mouth and tell me to drink up. It was good for me, he would say, and it would keep the 'flu away. I did as I was told because I didn't want to get a wallop for disobeying him.

Sally asked if I knew how old I would have been at the time and I told her that I must have been between five and seven, because he died when I was eight. He was ill for a long time before he passed away. I believe he had stomach cancer, as I had heard them talk about it in the house the odd time and I recall him going into hospital for an operation. It's funny how you remember certain things from your childhood. I clearly remember them saying something about the fact that the doctors, after opening him up to operate, had found that the cancer had spread and so they had done what they could and sent him home to die.

I told Sally that I was confused by the thoughts I was having. I wasn't really sure if he had abused me. I couldn't remember him having sex with me; just the fact that I would hurt everywhere on the mornings after I had slept with him.

Sally looked at me with compassion in her eyes and said, "Ann, from what you have described to me, you most definitely were being abused when you were a child. You are not able to remember the actual abuse because the whiskey would have knocked you out and in a way that was a good thing for you."

I went on to tell her about the horrible discharge that I'd had from my vagina as a child from a very young age. It smelled and looked terrible. When I was around seventeen I went to work in Dublin and as I was leaving the house my foster mother said to me, "When you are up there go and get that problem seen to."

I explained to Sally that I was surprised by this comment because at first I didn't know what she meant by "that problem", so I asked her out straight.

She just said, "You know damn well what problem. The one that has smelled for years." And with that she turned back into the house and closed the door.

I told Sally that I had thought my foster mother never knew about the discharge, but reflecting on it now, she obviously had known all the time, just like I think she knew about everything else but chose to ignore it. I told Sally that as soon as my periods started I had terrible problems with them. They were really heavy and went on for nearly two weeks at a time and would leave me absolutely drained. But

I was never taken to a doctor or a specialist to sort it out. It too was swept under the carpet in the hope that it might just go away.

In Dublin I went to a GP and he gave me an appointment to see a gynaecologist, which I did, and within a week I was admitted to St Michael's Hospital in Dun Laoghaire. As I was under twenty-one, someone had to come in to sign the forms to allow me to have an anaesthetic. My foster mother must have got the people I was working for to come in and sign because she never came to see me.

When I came around after the operation the doctors told me that my womb and cervix were badly damaged – spilt in two and tilted to one side – and asked if I knew how it got that way. I told them that I had no idea, but I am sure they must have been thinking that I was very sexually active. Or maybe they suspected abuse and didn't know what to do about it. I'll never know. Back then people tended to sweep things like abuse under the carpet, simply because it was the unmentionable and no one – even professionals like doctors – knew what to do or how to deal with it. It was a taboo subject, best left alone. They told me it was unlikely I would be able to have children. They had done everything possible to repair the damage.

At seventeen I had no idea what they were on about; I was very "green" in more ways than one. I most certainly was not promiscuous. Liam was the first man I had sex with so what they told me in the hospital did not make any sense to me at the time and I never let it bother me. At least they got rid of the discharge that I had and the heavy periods stopped, which made my life a lot easier.

Years later, when I did have my first child, I wrote home to my foster mother and told her about the difficulties I'd had with my pregnancy and that I could not give birth naturally and had to have a caesarean. She wrote back and said, "I could have told you that years ago."

Now, I said to Sally, "Told me what? That her father had abused me and now I have to deal with the aftermath of it all?"

I told Sally that I felt very angry and totally lost. I had blamed myself for everything that had happened in my life, including the abuse by my grandfather. I was always told I was a "bad" girl and in my mind I must have done something for him to abuse me. Maybe I just wasn't good enough? Maybe I did something bad that I couldn't remember?

I also felt the same way about my marriage – that feeling of not being good enough or that, maybe if I had tried harder, or was a better person, Liam would not have been an alcoholic.

I told her that I sometimes wished I had never been born because, from the moment I entered into this big bad world, nobody wanted me.

And that is really how I felt – like a "stray", a "nobody", living my life and blaming myself simply for being born. Only now am I beginning to realise that it was actually the people in my life, and those who weren't but should have been, who made my life hellish.

Right at that very moment speaking to Sally I hated everybody around me, with the exception of my children.

Sally was my saving grace in many ways. She told me time and time again that nothing that had happened to me back then was my fault. She made me realise that I was simply an innocent child caught up in something I had absolutely no control over. She told me this in every session I had with her until I finally accepted it myself. She also made me realise that I was not to blame for Liam's drinking or his death. Those were the choices he made for himself. There were many things that Sally taught me and the simplest – yet the hardest of them all for me – was how to love myself, to be proud of who and what I am and to always realise that sometimes things happen that we have no control over and we just get through them as best we can. Without the help of Sally I would not have been able to find Ann, the Ann that I am today. And for that I am truly grateful.

SALLY

When I came to you, my life was a box.
Of cupboards and doors with all of them locked.
But somehow you found the key to open
All these cupboards and doors to years of emotions.
Then out came the anger, hurt, guilt and shame.
But it was you who taught me that I wasn't to blame.
You sat quietly with me when I could not speak
And you picked me up when I felt so weak.
You showed me how to look ahead
And taught me how to love myself.

* * *

Before I left my counsellor that day I knew in my heart that I was going to go back to Ireland to confront my foster mother and hopefully begin the search for my birth mother. Now, more than ever, I felt a longing to find this woman, to feel her arms around me, telling me she was sorry and that everything would now be okay.

So in August 2001 I took a plane from Stansted Airport to Dublin. I was feeling very apprehensive because I didn't know what lay ahead. My main worry was seeing my foster mother again and challenging her to come clean about my childhood.

I hired a car at Dublin Airport but it was a nightmare finding my way out of Dublin because the capital had changed so much over the years. I was going to stay at Tricia's house as she and her family had moved back to Ireland after their first child was born. They had built a lovely home near the village where she was raised, and Bridie, Tricia's mother, went to live with them and stayed there until she sadly passed away.

I finally arrived at Tricia's house late in the afternoon, totally exhausted. After receiving a very warm welcome from Tricia and her family and a much appreciated cup of tea, I sat debating whether I should go to see my foster mother that evening or the next morning. The more I thought about going the sicker I felt, worrying about how she would receive me.

I kept telling myself, *Snap out of it, Ann, you're a grown woman of fifty-one acting like a child* – and that's when it hit me. I was actually frightened for the child within me and I didn't know if I was strong enough to protect her this time, or the woman she had grown into. I thought, *Oh God, how I wish I had someone to lean on right now.* But I decided that if I put it off again I'd never do it.

I wasn't sure if she knew I was in the area already and I just hoped that no one had told her because word gets around so quickly in our little village and everyone looks for something to gossip about. I parked the car and walked up to the gate, my stomach turning. I knocked at the door and when she finally opened it I noticed immediately how old she had got and how grey her hair had become. She didn't recognise me at first, mainly because I had lost a lot of weight. I had always been fat and, dear God, did she let me know it! However, standing before her now was a different woman, a much slimmer and well-dressed woman who, I hoped with all my heart, had the strength, courage and confidence to go through with what she had travelled all this way for.

"It's me – Rossie." I hated having to say that name, but it was the only name she would use to me.

I could feel my stomach heaving and the child within me quivering when she said, "Jesus, Rossie, I hardly knew you. What have you done to yourself? What happened to all the fat that was on you?"

"Oh, I got rid of some of it."

"And about bloody time too."

I waited for her to invite me in, which she did. We went into the living area, which used to be the kitchen when I was a child. As I looked around at how the house had gone downhill I felt a pang of guilt, knowing that the few meagre luxuries I saw around this little place were all she had left in her life. I had to check myself for feeling sorry for her. She had lost her whole family in the previous twenty years. Her two daughters Kate and Nancy both died young. Kate was only thirty-five, I think, and Nancy was forty-four. Jimmy, her husband and my dad, died the same year as Kate back in 1981. Everything and everyone she had was gone. I meant nothing to her and unfortunately I was all that she had left in this world. She was now living more or less as a recluse, apart from the help of one solid friend who had been her pal for as long as I could remember. He would take her shopping and do whatever he could for her and I think she relied on him more than she cared to admit.

As usual I found it very hard to make conversation with her. From where I was sitting, I was looking straight down the hallway. Once again it was like *déjà vu*; all I could see was that young innocent little girl leaning against the wall with her hands behind her back. It was like looking back into the past. I could see myself as a pretty little four-year-old lying on my back, having just been walloped with a shovel; and as an eight-year-old, being forced to sprinkle holy water over my grandfather's body in his coffin while telling him that I was sorry for being a bad girl – and being told that I was the cause of him dying. I thought, *If walls could talk, what a story they would tell.*

I could feel my emotions welling up and I tried hard to stifle them. The last thing I wanted to do was to break down in front of this woman.

I wanted to get up and wander through the house and the rooms to rid myself of the fears I had around them, but I didn't have the courage to do it. She would have told me that I was a bloody nosy cow and I didn't want to stir up any ill feelings right now. I knew that I was already treading on eggshells around her and I wanted to get as much information from her as I possibly could.

The one thing I did notice, though, was how small the house actually was: it reminded me of the house in the Hansel and Gretel story. However, I quickly realised that the house was in fact just the same as it always had been; it was just that I had grown up. I was no longer the child, but God, did I feel so sorry for that child who felt abandoned by everyone around her.

We sat and chatted for a while and then I decided to come straight out and ask what I needed. "Mother, I would like to ask you if you know anything about my birth mother."

She wasn't happy with my questioning and said, "What do you want to go nosing around that for? It makes no difference now, so why can't you just leave it alone?"

"It makes a lot of difference to me. It would help if you could tell me as much as you can about it." I told her that I had always wanted to know who my mother was, and who my children's biological grandmother was, as I always felt alone in this world and needed to find out as much as I could about myself.

I had never approached my foster mother on this matter before, as I was always to scared to do so. After giving me a lecture about leaving well enough alone she eventually began to open up. She told me that my birth mother had given me away to some woman when I was only a tiny baby and she (my birth mother) supposedly told this woman that she would pay her to look after me. Seemingly, though, my birth mother never did pay her.

"But who was this woman?" I asked her.

"As far as I know," she told me, "it was a gypsy who was passing by, or it could have been some stranger. I'm not sure."

"How old was I when you took me in?"

"You were two."

I was taken aback by this. "But you told me before that I was the child in the wicker basket behind the door in the middle bedroom?"

"Yes," she replied, "I told you that already."

But if I was two, I thought, *was I not much too big for a basket?*

She went on to tell me how neglected I was when she got me. "You were covered from head to toe in welts and blisters and you had burns and bruises all over your body. I've no idea who treated you like that and I never asked."

"Did you get me from the County Home?"

"Yes," she said, to my surprise.

"Surely the Home would not allow me to be fostered in such conditions? Would they not have found out who did it? Are there any medical records to validate this?"

She started to get irritated at this stage and I could see her mood changing as she snapped, "How the hell do I know?"

I didn't push her as I could see her face was getting

redder by the minute and I didn't want the conversation to go sour on me. I decided I would come back and see her before I returned to London. For now, I needed time to think, as there were a lot of questions going around in my head that needed answers.

The biggest one was, who had treated me that way, and why? Was it the woman that my mother gave me to? Was it the Home? Or was it in fact my foster mother herself? She was definitely capable of it, as I knew only too well. Surely someone should know something? I did know that I still bore some of the hallmarks on my spine from being either neglected or abused – you could actually put your little finger into the hole that I have at the end of my spine. I was once told by a doctor that the spinal damage may have been the result of being left in soiled and wet nappies as a baby; the end of my spine could have gone septic from this.

And then what my foster mother had said about the neglect dawned on me, and I thought, *Maybe that was how I remembered the wicker basket* – because I must have been two or three years old when I slept in this basket. If I had been so neglected I was probably very small, underweight and underdeveloped and therefore, I suppose, I could have fitted into this basket. It was as if a weight had been lifted off my shoulders as I started piecing things together. Finally I could start to understand the puzzle over the wicker basket, all those years later.

I asked her if she knew anything about my biological father. She said that as far as she knew he was a teacher. I didn't know whether this was true or not because, if she didn't know very much about my mother, how would she know about my father? I knew nothing whatsoever about him, not even his name.

I was starting to feel stressed out and I could feel everything getting in on me. I knew that I needed some time and space to think about things. I never really knew what to believe from my foster mother so I was also taking everything she said with a pinch of salt, so to speak.

I still didn't have the courage to speak to her about the abuse. I just wasn't able to cope with any more information at that time. I felt so lost and alone all of a sudden and I just wanted to get out.

So I left my foster mother and went back to Tricia's, where we sat and talked about what went on back at the house. We had a long chat about the past and Tricia told me that she remembered my mother trying to smother me in a bucket of water one day. She said she had never liked my mother and she couldn't understand how my foster parents had got away with the abuse for so long. I was shocked at this because she had never mentioned it before but she said she knew how hard it was for me to cope with everything else and she didn't want to make it any worse by telling me before this.

She said everyone in the village spoke about the treatment I received, yet nothing was done. And to think that up until then I thought it had all gone unnoticed.

* * *

Before I arrived in Ireland I had originally started to research my roots through the internet, with a fellow in the

US called Tony. It was through him that I was now going to meet a woman called Helen, who had direct links to my mother. It appears that Helen's uncle had married my mother, so in fact her uncle is my stepfather. I had written to Helen before I left London to say that I was coming to Ireland. She had told me my mother was called Agnes Foley. I phoned her from Tricia's house that evening. She asked if I would meet her as she had something to tell me, which she would only do if she saw me face to face when I came back to my home county. So I arranged to meet Helen on the 10th of August.

I spent much of my time in the days leading up to the meeting relaxing and chatting with Tricia and her family. I had always felt so relaxed with them over the years and being around them took my mind off things. One night I went down to the pub in my old village and I met a lot of people who knew me when I was a child. Tricia introduced us all and I was amazed at some of the things they told me. These were some of the people whom I was never allowed to speak to when I was growing up, obviously for fear of what they might tell me or me them. However, they all knew what was going on. I realised that there was a life going on in this village that I never knew about, or was never allowed to take part in, and that really hurt.

One of the men in the pub was Pat, a man I have known nearly all of my life, who is about seven or eight years older than me. Pat told me what my grandfather did to me when I was about six years old at the water pump, which was situated across the road from our house. Pat said that he was at the pump getting water at the same time as my grandfather and I. "You didn't pump the water hard enough, Ann, so he picked you up by the scruff of the neck and spat into your eyes with his tobacco spit and you screamed in pain." My grandfather had then turned away from me, ignoring the fact that I was in pain, and he had walked back to the house leaving me crying.

I was speechless when I heard this. I couldn't understand why anyone would want to do that to a defenceless child. Hearing such stories made me feel so angry and frustrated because there was nothing I could do about it. It proved to me that all of the abuse, mentally and physically, had in fact all happened just as I had remembered; yet those who hurt and abused me had walked away scot-free.

I also found out that some of the neighbours had alerted the authorities to what was happening to me when I was living there. They told me that they had always felt something was "not right" in my house. They all saw with their own eyes how differently I was treated to the other girls in the family. On a few occasions, I believe social workers were sent to the house and met with mother, asking how things were going with me. According to the old neighbours, including Tricia's family, mother would tell the social workers that all was well, and seemingly a glass of whiskey would be plonked onto the table and the social worker would leave our home in good spirits.

I never remember seeing anyone like this in the house because I was probably kept well out of the way for these little visits. In all the years I was there I never met with any of them. I was never told they called and I have never been able to find out anything else about these calls. But seemingly that's how she kept her little secret hidden. I'm sure she hated everyone in the village knowing that there was someone spilling the beans on her every now and then.

I was also told that a few strange people used to come to try and see me during the summer months, but I was never there. I took it from this explanation that these people were possibly members of my mother's or my father's family who may have wanted to check that I was okay with my foster parents. Of course, I had never been told any of this by the Nolans. This reminded me of the summers I spent with my foster cousins, and my encounter when I was twelve with the man outside the pub who had told me my name was Áine. I suspected that this man was one of my father's relatives who used to try to visit me. Perhaps my foster parents sent me away specifically so I wouldn't meet these visitors, but chance had made me cross paths with one of them that day.

* * *

I spent a lot of time that week, as I waited for my meeting with Helen, chatting with Tricia, reminiscing about some of the nice old people in the village and how the two of us always seemed to have a laugh, even when I was at my lowest ebb.

Then, on what turned out to be my birthday, I headed off to meet Helen for a coffee and a chat. And what a day it turned out to be!

The two of us hit it off straight away. She told me that I looked nothing like my birth mother. She had met her many times. She told me that we were going to drive over to Bob's house; Bob was a man who had helped me with some research, and he had also asked to meet me when I came home.

When we finally arrived at his house Bob invited us both in and I met his wife, who kindly made us some tea. During the course of the visit Bob kept looking at me and smiling. Eventually I asked him if he was going to let me in on the joke: "You have been quietly smiling to yourself since I walked in; what's so funny?"

"Ann, as soon as I saw you get out of your car I knew who you were. There is no mistaking it; you are the walking image of your father."

I was stunned. "My father," I said. "You know my father!"

"Yes, I knew your father well and you, Ann, are just like him – you sit like him, you walk like him and all your mannerisms are just like his."

"What is his name?" I replied.

"Do you not know his name?" Bob asked.

"No, I have no idea what his name is, never mind who he is, as I have never been told anything about him. My foster mother thinks he may have been a teacher or something."

"His name was Michael Brophy," Bob said. "He was from the same town as your mother."

"Michael . . . Michael . . . Michael," I kept repeating the name over and over in my head. I couldn't believe that after all these years I had a name for my father.

"Bob, you say he *was* from the same town as my mother. Does that mean he is no longer alive?"

"Sadly, he died many years ago," he said. After a moment,

he went on, "Ann, Michael was a married man when you were born and he had a very young child, a son called Sean, who would be your half-brother. Your father had a threshing machine and used to go around to the farms in the area when it was time to harvest the wheat and barley." So he was not the teacher that my foster mother thought he was. "That was how I think he met your mother. He would have gone to your mother's farm as her father sowed wheat."

I could hardly believe what I was hearing. I was trying very hard to take it all in. Not only had I found out who my father was, but I had also discovered that I had a half-brother who would be a year older than me. I was totally flabbergasted.

Bob went on to tell me that my father came from a well-respected family and was well known and well liked in the area. He had eight brothers and sisters.

It seemed, as I had thought, that I was the result of too much booze on the night of the harvest. Seemingly my father had a brief fling with my mother, a one-night stand, and *voilà*: nine months later I popped out. Bob went on to say that my father knew only too well that I had been born and he made no secret of it. However, it did destroy his relationship with his family.

I sat looking at Bob in this cosy kitchen of his with his wife by his side, trying hard to keep my emotions in check. Hearing all of this was more than I could ever have possibly dreamed of.

Helen and Bob told me so much about my lost family. Helen told me about the day my mother got married to her husband, as she herself had been at the wedding, which happened five years after I was born. This man – Helen's uncle – was also a farmer and it seems that when he died my mother sold the farm and drank most of the money. She had a serious drink problem. They believed that she was still alive, and lived in another county, just a few miles from where we were sitting.

I tried hard to hold back the tears as I was told how my mother's husband knew about my birth. It seemed that everyone in their little close-knit community was aware of the child born out of wedlock.

I was also devastated when I heard that my real father was dead. I felt so upset that I had never had the chance to meet him. I wondered if in fact it was my father who used to call to the village looking for me in the summer months when I was a child. I felt so low at that moment but I held onto the fact that, despite this horrible news, it was possible that I would soon meet my natural mother.

Before we left, Bob turned to me and said, "Ann, it has been a great honour to meet you. You are such a lovely person and I believe that your father would have been very proud of you."

At that stage I nearly choked on the tears that were welling up inside me. I tried desperately to keep my composure, but Bob knew how I was feeling as he came over and gave me a hug.

* * *

I left that farmyard with a thousand questions running through my head. I didn't want to plague Helen with all my questions; she must have been in her seventies and I didn't want to put too much pressure on her.

Helen told me that she wanted to take me to a graveyard next. When we arrived at the church, we found the grave of my maternal grandparents. I knelt and said some prayers, which felt strange, as I was looking at the names of two people who were my real grandparents but whom I never knew, nor they me.

Helen also went to the grave of her own parents that day and as she was saying some prayers I wandered around looking at other gravestones. Then I suddenly spotted my father's name engraved on a headstone. His date of death in 1974 was just four weeks before my first daughter, his granddaughter, was born. I had been overcome with the stories Bob and Helen had just told me about him and now finding his resting place became too much for me to take in. I fell to my knees in tears and a few minutes later Helen walked across to me and led me away.

I felt quite weak, so we found a tea room and I was able to calm down a bit. To be certain, I asked Helen if that had in fact been the grave of my father and she said it was. "I'm sorry, Ann," she said. "I didn't realise that he was buried there; I've never seen his grave before. If I'd known I would have told you before you saw it for yourself."

"Don't worry about it, Helen. It was obviously meant to happen as it did."

Before we left I went back and took some pictures of his headstone; it would be the only physical proof I would ever have about who my father was.

The father who lived so near and was yet so far away.

* * *

Our next stop was to meet a lovely woman called Maura, who had been at school with my mother, but was in a class below her. Maura told me that I was a very nice lady. All of these people were telling me how nice I was and yet I could never see anything nice in myself. Maura told me more about my mother. She didn't have a bad word to say about her. My mother's mother – my natural grandmother – had died when my own Mam was very young, leaving her father to bring her up with her brother on their farm.

I was still sitting there in shock because, within a couple of hours, I had found out who both my mother and my father were and had names for both. Neither name had been listed on my birth cert. It felt very weird and unreal, to say the least. I was trying to retain everything I was being told to avoid forgetting things later.

I asked Maura if she knew how old my mother would have been when I was born. When she told me that she had been nearly thirty I almost fell off the chair. I had always assumed that she must have been only sixteen or seventeen and gave me away simply because she was unable to cope with being a single mother in a small town. I was in total shock so I asked Maura, "Are you sure that was her age when she had me?"

"Yes, I'm sure," said Maura.

Helen added, "Thirty would have been about right because she married my uncle when she was in her mid-thirties. That was about five years after she had you, Ann, and she went on to have another daughter after that."

Now I not only had a mother and a father but also a half-sister and a half-brother on two separate sides of my family tree.

We talked some more and Maura told me that I looked a lot like my father's side of the family. Try as they might, neither of them could see anything of my mother in my features or my personality. Maura said that she had to go but she wished me well in my search for my roots. I told her, "It feels very odd that I came here to look for my mother and instead I found out so much about my father, which I didn't expect. I had no idea who he was or where he came from before I arrived."

I thanked her for all her help and said that Helen would let her know if anything should come of any of it.

* * *

We drove back to Helen's house and had some supper. I only had something light to eat as I was going out for a meal with my friend Tricia as it was my birthday. I got the feeling that Helen didn't want me to leave; I had felt this with Bob and with Maura as well. It was very odd. I think they were keen for me to reach the end of my search and felt obliged to do as much as possible to help me get there. But I felt that I needed to get away that night. I'd had more than I could take for one day and I had a lot to think about.

The drive back to Tricia's did not take long and my mind was racing with questions, most of which I had no answers to.

Tricia was shocked when I told her how eventful the last

few hours had been, after spending fifty-one years of my life in the dark about my past. I went into town with her and her two daughters and we had a lovely Indian meal and talked and talked about the day that had just gone. I felt drained, but surprisingly happy. Exhausted, I slept well that night.

The next day I took things easy. I didn't want to race into anything so I decided to relax and take a bit more time to gather my thoughts. I was considering the best way of approaching my birth mother. I knew that simply knocking on the woman's door may not have been a great idea for either of us. I regretted not having brought one of my children over with me for support. I had told them the broad outline of the story on the phone the night before. They were shocked but delighted, knowing that I had finally begun to find the real me.

I was terrified now that I would fall to pieces if my mother disowned me. My mind was all over the place.

I called into my foster mother that morning but I decided not to say too much about what had happened the day before. However, I did say that I had found out who my father was. She got very annoyed at this. "Ah, that's all lies. Don't you mind the lies that people are telling you."

I looked at her and said, "I thought you would be pleased for me, at least for once in your life."

I turned to walk out the door. I felt that this was the last straw and that there was no point in even trying to talk to her. She asked me where I was going and without thinking I told her I was going into town. She immediately asked if she could come along and, unfortunately for me, I foolishly agreed.

The trip would have been lovely but she did nothing but complain all the way there and back. We went into a restaurant for a bite to eat and she was so rude to the staff that I ended up returning to apologise for her behaviour after I had put her back into the car.

I decided not to ask her anything that day about my childhood or the abuse by my grandfather. I was unable to voice the words and I was scared of what her reaction might be.

I felt that she was trying to destroy what I had found out about my father, which really upset me. I thought, *Could she not for once be happy for me and not be so damned spiteful?* But I suppose that would have been asking too much from her. I was never so glad to drop anyone off as I was her that day.

* * *

The following morning I got up early and set out to try to find my mother.

I wasn't exactly sure where she lived but I drove to the town where Maura believed she had moved to. It was a very hot day but I eventually found the place and parked the car in the village. Only then did it dawn on me that I had been so eager just to get to this place, I hadn't even thought about what I would do once I got there. As I sat in the car thinking, I saw the sign for the post office across the road. Maybe they would know if she came in here for her pension or something? They might tell me where she lived. I went into the post office, absolutely shaking; one part of me wanted to know and the other part wanted to run away.

I asked the man behind the counter if he knew an Agnes Foley, adding, "I think she lives with her daughter and granddaughter." Maura had told me this.

"I know of her all right," he said, "and I know where she lived – but she moved about three years ago." He didn't know where she went but he suggested I talk to the parish priest, who lived down the road just opposite the junction. "Sure he knows everything!"

I got into the car and drove the short distance to the parochial house. As I was pulling into his drive, the priest was standing at the door waving to me. I thought this a little strange, but reckoned the man in the post office had rung and told him to expect me. That's small towns for you.

He invited me in and promptly put the kettle on. He hadn't even asked me who I was at this stage. While we were waiting for the kettle to boil he said, "I believe you are looking for Agnes Foley?"

"Yes, this town is the last address I have for her," I told him.

"I don't know where she moved to, but I'll do what I can to help you find her." He went on to confirm what the man in the post office had told me – that she had moved about three years ago – "I think it was because she had got into some financial difficulty with the rent. Betty, her daughter, and her granddaughter went with her."

I must have been sitting there for well over half an hour when a thought struck me. We had been talking for all this time and he hadn't even asked me who I was or what business I had with this woman. Then, as if reading my mind, he said, "Can I ask, are you related to her?"

Maybe because he was a priest, I decided to be honest. "I believe she is my mother."

He calmly replied, "Well, if that is the case we will do our very best to find out where she moved to. And I think I know where to start."

"That's very kind of you," I said. "Are you sure? I don't want to be putting you to any bother."

"No bother at all. Come on, we'll take my car. Yours will be quite safe left here." And with that he started to walk towards the front door, beckoning me to follow him.

We set off down the road. Every time he saw someone he knew he would stop the car right in the middle of the road and get out to speak to them. Being a priest, I assumed he would be a safe driver, but he was driving all over the place! I thought, *Well, if I die trying, I will surely have a free pass into heaven with this guy.*

He stopped on a bend in the road and got out to chat with a woman across the road. I prayed, *Please God, don't let a car come up too fast behind us or I will be killed instantly.* Thankfully nothing did.

We must have spent well over an hour driving all around the area, with no success. No one knew where she had moved to, not even the schoolteacher. I could feel that he was getting a little despondent so I said, "Listen, Father, I am very grateful for all your help and I don't want you to be wasting any more of your time." But he wouldn't have any of it, so we continued on. He was determined to reunite me with my long-lost mother.

He said, "She can't have just disappeared off the face of the earth."

We drove back to the village and he stopped at the shop at the end of the road. And as sure as there is a God in heaven, the shopkeeper knew where my mother had moved to. In fact, he had an address for her. I couldn't help thinking, *Imagine – all this could have been solved right at the beginning if we had only walked across the road and asked this man!* But then again, I would have missed the magical mystery tour given by the mad local parish priest.

When we got back to where my car was parked outside the parochial house, I said, "Thank you so much for all your help, Father. I couldn't have done it without you."

"Not at all! Good luck, God bless, and have a safe journey."

* * *

I set off for the next stage of my voyage of discovery still filled with a great deal of anxiety. I was going into unknown territory and wasn't sure what to expect. For that matter, I didn't even know if I would find her at home.

During the drive I reflected on how kind and helpful everybody had been in the town. They didn't have to be, but they were, and I will be forever grateful to them for it.

I eventually arrived at what I hoped was my final destination at around two in the afternoon. I felt very tired and wondered if I was doing the right thing. I could feel my insides churning and knew I needed something to eat but felt too sick to even contemplate food. I found the street address that I had been given and parked the car. I needed to think deeply about what I was going to say.

I felt that I needed some reassurance and a little moral support, so I decided to ring my good friend Christine in London before I went to look for my mother's house. I was beginning to lose my courage to go through with it. In fact I was so frazzled, I don't know how I even managed to drive there without crashing into something.

I eventually managed to get through to her from a call box in the local supermarket. I told her about everything that had happened. I told her that I was near my mother's house and that I didn't know what to do next. But I knew in my heart that even if she didn't want to see me, I needed to get her to confirm that my father was who everyone had said he was.

I also wanted to see her face, to have a picture in my mind of her. I prayed that she would answer all my questions and that she would welcome me with open arms. I knew that nothing could be taken for granted, though: she had left me all alone, abandoned me, when she was a grown adult, instead of facing up to reality and rearing her child. Even if she felt she couldn't give me all I needed, it would have been a lot better than what I was lumbered with instead.

I told Christine all of these hopes and fears. She simply listened and said, "Ann, you have come so far. Try to find that extra bit of courage to see it through; otherwise you will regret it."

I thanked Christine for listening to me, hung up the phone and went back to my car. I knew she was right, but would I be able to get that extra bit of courage? I felt so scared and frightened. I realised that I hadn't prepared myself mentally for any outcome to this visit.

I sat in the car for a minute or two reciting the first line of the Serenity Prayer we say in Al-Anon – "God, grant me the serenity to accept the things I cannot change" – because I knew that whatever happened with my mother I would have to accept it. With that thought in my head I got out of the car and went to look for the door number, only to find that I had parked the car directly across the road from her front door.

Here goes, I thought, as I put my shaking finger on the doorbell and pressed.

* * *

It felt like an eternity but it must have been less than a minute before the door was opened. Before me stood an old woman. She had very grey hair and a long face. It looked as if she had been in an accident at some time, but I now know that she had Bell's Palsy.

I immediately saw a shock of recognition registering on her face.

I asked her, "Are you Agnes Foley?"

"Yes, I am."

I took a deep breath, ready to tell her who I was, "I'm–"

But she abruptly interrupted me. "I know who you are."

"Pardon?"

"I know who you are, so don't bother telling me," she snapped.

"How do you know who I am?"

"You're her," she said.

"Are you quite sure you know who I am?"

"Yes – you're her."

"Who's her?" I asked.

She couldn't say or wouldn't say, so I said, "I'm Ann."

"All right then, so you are," she replied.

By this time I was feeling so sick I could have thrown up. She stepped back and beckoned for me to come in. I could tell she was mortified. When I stepped inside into the hall my heart dropped. I was shocked to see that she seemed to be living in squalor. I found it hard to take in. I felt deeply sorry for her before we had even spoken.

She seemed to be alone in the house. I took it that her daughter Betty was out at work or shopping and her little girl would have probably been in school.

Before I sat down to talk I asked her if I could use her bathroom. She told me that it was beside the kitchen. If I thought the front room was bad, nothing could have prepared me for the bathroom, if you could call it that. The toilet itself wobbled and the drainpipe looked loose. I was very uncomfortable even standing in the room, never mind using the toilet. When I had finished I went to wash my hands but couldn't find anything clean to dry them on, so I wiped my hands down the sides of my trousers.

I joined her in the kitchen. She was making tea by boiling the water in a teapot on top of the gas stove. The kitchen was small, cramped and dirty. She handed me a mug of tea; she had put sugar in it without asking me if I take sugar (I don't), but I took it without complaining. I waited for her to sit down before I spoke.

I started off by apologising to her about landing on her

doorstep unexpectedly, but somehow I had a feeling that she knew I was coming and looking for her.

We chatted for a while, and she told me a little about herself. For some reason, she talked to me a lot about the day her mother had died, seventy years earlier.

Finally, I steered the conversation back to the purpose of my visit. I told her why I had come after all these years. "I've always felt my life was like a jigsaw puzzle with a lot of missing pieces, and I'm trying to fill in or find those missing pieces. I'm hoping that you might be able to help me do that." I paused. "Do you ever think about me?"

She simply replied, "Sometimes."

"It must have been very hard for you to give me up when you kept me for so long."

"I didn't keep you for very long and I didn't have a problem in giving you up," she replied.

"What do you mean?" I asked. "How old was I when you gave me up?"

"You were two weeks old. And I didn't give you up – I gave you away to a woman called Mary Dooley. She was a gypsy woman who moved around a lot. I never saw you or her again as she moved away from the area."

This threw me a little, as I had been led to believe that she had kept me for nine months, and had built up a bond with me. Quietly, I asked her, "Why did you give me away?"

"I didn't like you or want you and I didn't care if I never saw you again when I gave you away."

I sat in that dirty kitchen looking at the woman who had carried me for nine months – my biological mother – telling me that she neither liked me nor wanted me. She may just as well have got a knife and cut my heart out right there and then. I could feel my heart weeping with her words, spoken without a hint of remorse. I was left shaking with the shock of it all.

The child within me wanted to scream at her, *Why, why didn't you like me? Was I that ugly?* I had been crying out to be loved and wanted by this woman all of my life, a woman I had never known anything about but whom I had assumed felt the same about me. Now she sat there, hard as nails, telling me that she gave me away to a gypsy woman because she didn't want me, or like me. Was she that desperate to get rid of me?

I wanted the ground to open up and swallow me; I would have willingly fallen into it. I was heartbroken, numb, weak and sick. I didn't know what to do or say. But I knew that I could not let her see how much she had hurt me. Something inside of me kicked in – a stubbornness and a determination to see this through, as I knew it was my last chance.

I asked her about the name she had given me. "You gave me a lovely name. I have often wondered where you got it from. Can you remember what it is?"

"No, I don't remember what name I gave you. I can't even remember if I did give you one. I wasn't worried about giving you one."

This woman was able to tell me everything about the day her mother had died seventy years earlier, but she could not remember the day I was born or the name she had given me.

Again her answers and attitude shook me, but I ploughed on, "Surely you remember the name you gave me, even if you didn't like me or want me?"

"And what name would that be, then?"

"Anastasia."

"Oh, that," she said. "When I first looked at you I thought you were lovely and the name just came to my head. I thought that it would do you."

"Do you know who my father was?" I asked her.

This question took her by surprise, but I needed to know and I had gone past the line of caring anymore about what I asked her.

"I can't remember who he was, that was a long time ago."

"You must remember who he was, surely?"

I needed her to confirm my father's name, as she would be the only person able to do this.

"Oh yes, now I know who he was. Michael Brophy . . . yes, Michael Brophy."

It was the name I had wanted to hear, but somehow at that moment it meant nothing to me. My head was filled with her words. She had rejected me as a baby and now she had done it again. The feeling of rejection was overpowering.

I realised sitting in that kitchen that this woman, whom I had spent nearly thirty years of my life thinking about, praying that she would come to find me, did not have a single ounce of love or compassion for me. In fact, I think she despised me either for who I was or what I represented to her. Something must have gone seriously wrong for this woman all those years ago. As far as I could see, I was the result of that. It was obvious that, fifty-odd years on, she still held utter bitterness and resentment towards me.

We said nothing for a while, just sat there quietly, and

then she asked me if I was married and if I had children. I told her that I was a widow with three children.

"So you know what it is like to be on your own, then."

Little did she know that I had felt "on my own" all my life, whether I was married or not.

I decided to show her the photographs I had taken of my kids and myself. "These are your grandchildren, but you will never meet them," I told her. I felt bitchy saying this, but I had nothing left to lose.

She sat up a bit and, surprisingly, said, "They are very good-looking children. Can I keep these pictures?"

I felt like saying to her, *Yes, you can, on one condition, that you let me meet Betty, my half-sister.* Betty was born five years after she had abandoned me. But I bit my tongue. I just said that it was fine and she could have them.

Then she started talking about sending me money. Looking around at the squalor she was living in, I felt like asking her where she had hidden it, because she looked penniless to me. Her suggestion really got under my skin. I had come to that place looking for love and I felt like she was trying to pay me off to clear her own conscience.

"I didn't come here looking for anything from you," I said. "Nothing except information about my life. I don't need anything from you."

"Well, give me your address in London, anyway," she said.

"No, I don't want you to have my address."

She turned on me and said, "It's the bloody least you can do. I need it to sort things out with you."

"The least you can do" – the cheek of her, I thought. Aloud

I said, "There's nothing to sort and if you send me money I will just send it straight back to you."

But she wouldn't have any of it, so in the end I gave her the address.

Needless to say I have never heard a word from her since.

* * *

I left the house feeling devastated, confused and lost. I drove through a red light and nearly killed myself. I pulled in to the side of the road, shaking like a leaf. I was trying to think of where to go to get away from everything. I didn't want to go straight back to Tricia's because I felt my world had just fallen apart. All those years of hopes and dreams of eventually reuniting with my mother had been flushed down the drain in a matter of minutes.

My mind was in a whirl. I found it hard to believe that the woman I had just met was my mother. *There is no way on earth that I am like her*, I told myself repeatedly, *nor do I want to be*. Maybe I am like my father, as Bob had said to me. Who knows?

I had always felt that when we would finally meet, my mother and I, we would fall into each others' arms and the years that we had spent apart would all be wiped away in an instant. Those were the dreams that had kept me going throughout my life, the one ray of sunshine in my living hell. But now they had all been shattered into a million pieces, and I really didn't know what to do.

I wished then that I could just wash my face, blind my eyes and erase my memory, because at that very moment I really did not like who I was or what I was. Throughout my life I had felt that I had the word "bastard" written across my forehead, as everyone seemed to know what I was, but no one knew who I was. At that moment, I felt that I had lost my identity as quickly as I had found it.

By now, it was getting late in the evening. I decided to visit a park where Tricia, her cousin Diana and I had walked just days before. I drove to Diana's house to get directions to the park but when I got there she wasn't in. I headed into the village to see if I could spot her, but I didn't. I had no hope of finding the place, so I got back into my car, thinking to head for Tricia's house. Suddenly, I realised that I was parked outside a beautiful big church with lots of steps up to the door. I wondered if the doors were open, as it struck me as a good place to sit quietly with myself for a while. I decided to see if I was in luck.

Before I had come to Ireland I had gone to see a clairvoyant. Someone had recommended her to me a few years earlier, after Liam had died. I was very impressed with the outcome, so I went to see her again before my trip. She had told me a few things about my meeting with my mother that had turned out to be accurate. She had said the meeting would be hard and that I might not be happy with the outcome. She had also told me that I had a guardian angel looking after me, who had been there with me throughout my life. She told me that if I ever saw a white feather close to me I was to pick it up, as it was a sign that my guardian angel was near me. Now I take these sort of things with a pinch of salt, so I didn't pay much attention to what she said at the time.

Now, as I was walking up the steps to the church, I suddenly stopped. There on the step in front of me was a single but beautiful white feather. I looked around to see if there was a bird in the air before I bent and picked it up but there was nothing there. I took the feather in my hand and continued into the church.

I sat in that church for well over an hour with the white feather clutched firmly in my palm and I cried my eyes out. I had come to the end of the line and found nothing but rejection. I thought to myself how my whole life appeared to have been mapped out for me. It felt as though I was never meant to have any joy or luck. The only positive thing I had to cling onto was the thought of my beautiful children.

I found it hard to comprehend that my mother had completely abandoned me and didn't care if she never saw me again. Having a family of my own made it a lot harder to contemplate; even in my darkest hour, I could never abandon any of my children, no matter how hard life was.

I sat there in front of this beautiful altar with tears falling down my face, just clutching this little white feather, now soaked in salty tears. I prayed all that time, not for anyone or anything in particular. I lit some candles – one for the father I never knew and one for the mother who didn't want to know me.

I sat there with the feather in my hand and with questions that I now knew would never be answered running through my mind. I pondered on the fact that three women in my life had been given the task of loving and caring for a child – my birth mother, this gypsy woman and my foster mother – and each of them had failed me. I realised that I was thankful I hadn't turned out like any of them. I was Me, Ann. I was, and am, a strong woman. A woman who learned how to give love and accept love. I am a good mother and I was a good wife. Nobody taught me these things. Deep down I always knew what kind of person I was; I just had to let myself believe it.

Sitting there alone in the serenity of the church made me also think of all the trials and hardships I had endured in my life. I realised that no matter what I had gone through over the years I never ever gave up hope. My Faith and the hope that one day I would find the real me always kept me going. And finding the feather that day just made me believe even more that things were finally going to be okay.

It reminded me of a lovely card that one of my daughters gave me when I was going through a tough time, which had a beautiful story called "Footprints". It tells the tale of a man who had a dream that he was walking with God on the beach, and when he looked back he saw two sets of footprints in the sand. But he goes on to say that when he was going through his most troublesome times he noticed that there was only one set of prints in the sand. So he asked God why he had deserted him when he needed him the most. And God said, "My precious, precious child . . . it was then that I carried you." With that thought in my head and the feather in my pocket I walked out of that church and I knew that no matter what happened from here on in I would be able to cope.

* * *

Tricia was devastated when I told her what had happened that day, as were my own children when I phoned them. I don't know how I would have got through it all without them. I knew that I had to be strong and I knew that something or someone was there beside me keeping me going.

I went to meet Helen a couple of days later, before I headed back to London. She took me into the town where my half-brother lived and worked and although we didn't have much information about where we could find him, we decided to give it a try.

We found a shop with the name "Brophy" written over the door and I think we both assumed that this was it. Without saying anything to each other we walked in and the bell rang over the door as we entered. It was a very strange shop; we felt as if we had taken a step back in time to the 1950s or 1960s. There was a counter at the front and the customers would be served by the man behind it, who picked the things requested off the shelves. It reminded me of an old curiosity shop, the sort I would love to walk around, just browsing.

I called out "Hello?" a number of times, as there wasn't anyone about. Eventually a tall dark-haired man suddenly appeared from the bottom of the shop and said, "Hello. Can I help you?"

"I'm sorry to bother you," I replied, "but we are looking for a man called Sean Brophy. I noticed that's the surname over this shop, so I was wondering if it might be you I'm looking for?"

"It depends," he said. "Why are you looking for him?"

"I believe he may be my half-brother," I replied. I went on to tell him of my search, and that my half-brother on my father's side apparently worked in this town.

After hearing me out, he said, "I think I'm your cousin. I think my grandfather was your grandfather's brother." He ran upstairs and brought down a family tree. He continued to tell me some great stories about his family. He was full of information and I was amazed at his knowledge of his family.

I told him that he had a very old-fashioned shop and that I was wondering why he never changed it.

"I like it the way it is," he said, smiling. "I know where everything is."

We talked for a little longer and he told me that the man I was looking for could be his cousin, who worked in a shop not far away. He gave me directions, I thanked him and left.

I got to the shop where Sean worked, only to be told that he was on holiday. Luckily, though, the man in the shop gave me his mobile phone number. He never asked me who I was or why I wanted to speak to Sean – he just wrote the number down on a scrap of paper and handed it to me.

It was odd how things seemed to be working out for me on this trip more than ever before.

When I left the shop I stood in the middle of the square with the phone number in my hand, wondering what to do next. I knew that, whatever I chose to do, the next step I took on this epic journey was going to be mentally and emotionally difficult. I continued to stand and stare at the phone number for a few minutes. Helen kept telling me just to bite the bullet and ring him. But something inside me didn't want me to make that call yet. How would he feel finding out, literally out of the blue, that he had a half-sister and that his father had had sex with another woman while he was married? Would he think that someone was simply playing a practical joke on him and hang up the phone? There were so many scenarios going on in my head that I could hardly think straight. But time was running out for me, as I was going back to London the next day.

Finally I went into the phone box and, with shaking hands, I dialled the phone number. I nearly put the phone down, but then I heard a lovely Irish accent say, "Hello."

I said, "Hi, is this Sean?"

"It is."

I went on to tell him about what I was doing – about the research that I had done and the people I had met – and that I had been told that he was my half-brother. I said it all in a rush of words, and waited for him to respond. He said nothing for a minute and then, understandably, he started asking a lot of questions. He was shocked to hear that he had a half-sister, as he never knew I existed, but, as I said to him, nor did I know that he existed until that week.

"I'm sorry for landing this on you," I told him. "It was as much a shock to me as it must be to you."

I told him that I was on my way back to London the next morning and didn't have time to do any more research. We exchanged phone numbers and I told him I'd contact him from London in a week or two. He replied that he wanted to do some research as well and said that we should keep in touch.

After hanging up, I promptly burst into tears. I was

emotionally drained and shaking like a leaf. The impact of what I had just done hit me like a ton of bricks. I had spoken to a man who, if I had done my research right, was a living half-brother, a direct connection to my father, a father whose name I had only heard three or four days earlier. Now I had just spoken to his son, my half-brother. It was a weird conversation and the fact that it was over the phone probably made it even more so.

Helen threw her arms around me and I sobbed and sobbed. I went back to her house that night and had a lovely meal and tried to relax.

* * *

Later that evening I went with Tricia and her husband down to the village pub. Once again I met a lot of elderly local people who had known me as a child and who told me tales of my upbringing. Even though I had not said anything about it, I got the feeling that they knew that whenever I returned to the village it was to find out about myself.

I left the next day after a week-long emotional rollercoaster ride. On the flight back to London I thought over the week's events, trying to work out how I felt and wondering how much I was going to tell my own children and my friends when I touched down. I was not sure if I wanted to tell them the whole truth about my mother. I was finding it very hard to come to terms with what she had said to me. I was still feeling very emotional at how my meeting with my mother had turned out and I didn't want to have to explain to anyone or justify my feelings.

What can I say about my mother? I am confused about my feelings for her. I wanted so much that day to feel her arms around me. She didn't have to say anything; just her arms around me would have been enough. I would have forgiven her for anything. But if I have any feelings for her now it would have to be sorrow. I feel sorry for her because I know that she has carried all of this bitterness with her throughout her life. What hurt me the most was the uncaring attitude that she had shown towards me. But then, I have to look at my own expectations. Was I expecting her to welcome me with open arms and for her to tell me how sorry she was when she had to give me up? Deep down inside of me I know that is exactly what I was looking for – my mother's love. Being deprived of love from any adult throughout my life, I had pinned my hopes on my own mother giving me the love that I so desperately sought. I thought she would have been the one person who would have unconditionally accepted who I was.

Throughout my life I had been torn because I never knew anything about my origins. It hurt me more than anyone knew. I know that family and friends would say to me, "But we know who you are" – but it is not the same as knowing who I am myself. I had always felt that when I was in conversation with people talking about their families, my back was always up against the wall. I could go no further than myself. This always made me feel very uncomfortable. I would either end the conversation or walk away.

Meeting my mother had left me wondering whether the actual "knowing" was in fact worse than the "not knowing".

For years I had lived with my dreams of how things could have worked out, that possibly one day I would be reunited happily with my mother – and then suddenly all of those dreams were shattered into a million pieces, leaving me totally devastated. The idea of this mother figure that I had built up in my mind over the years and the dreams associated with that woman suddenly no longer existed. The half-sister that I would have loved to meet I would now never get to know. Sitting on the plane back to London, I couldn't help feeling that I had been a mistake that should not have happened. But what was done was done and I knew that I just had to accept it.

* * *

A few weeks after my scary phone call to my half-brother I arrived in Dublin to meet up with him for the very first time. I had sent him a picture of myself when I was only two or three years old by e-mail. It was the one and only picture I had of myself as a child. I didn't know what he would look like, nor him me, and I was very excited and nervous. We had been communicating over the weeks and he had done some research himself, which had confirmed everything for both of us.

I had arranged to meet him in the foyer of a Dublin city centre hotel. I saw a man walk into reception and I knew there and then, without any photos, that this man was indeed my half-brother. I approached him and said, "I'm Ann, and you have to be my brother."

He said, "Yes, I am, and it's lovely to meet you."

We looked at each other and smiled a smile that said everything without saying anything.

He led me into the lounge area where his wife and daughter were waiting. They had travelled up from the country to be with him.

We had the most wonderful meeting that anyone could ask for. He told me that I did indeed look like my father. He said that when I sent him the picture of myself as a child, he knew straight away that there was no mistake. He was one hundred per cent sure that I was who I said I was.

He told me a lot about our dad – what kind of a man he was and so on. He said that he had never been told about what had happened, but he knew something had. Every time my mother's name was mentioned in his house it caused trouble, but he could never understand why.

We talked a lot about how I had done my research, using the Internet and so on, and he told me that I was very brave in doing so. He also told me a lot about my mother's family and what kind of people they were, which I'm afraid was not all good. However, I had half-expected that from the way my mother behaved towards me.

While we were sitting at the table, I noticed that Sean and I had very similar habits, especially with our hands. I think Sean's wife noticed too; she said that she also had no doubt that we were related.

We spent three wonderful hours getting to know each other and we took quite a lot of photos of each other that day to put in our family albums. Sean left the hotel with his family that evening and my head felt like it was floating. I could hardly believe what had just happened. I wanted to talk about it and at the same time I didn't want to talk about it. What I would have really liked was some time on my own, but I knew that was not possible right then, as I had to get to the North Wall to get the boat back to Holyhead.

I was content now that I had finally met one member of my family who didn't turn me away. Finding that I had a half-brother was not what I had set out to do, but it was most definitely a bonus.

I never said it to him, but I will always be grateful to him, no matter what happens between us in the future, for agreeing to meet me and for not turning his back on me.

I only wish that his father, our father, could have been there beside us. And yet, maybe he was.

CHAPTER TWELVE

Full Circle

A good few years have now passed since I had that first meeting with my long lost half-brother in Dublin. About a year after our first get-together I went to Ireland and spent a wonderful week with him and his family in their home. Meeting so many aunts and uncles was unbelievable and very exciting. Everyone was so lovely and friendly toward me but I found the whole experience rather daunting. I was trying to keep my feelings under wraps as I met all these people; I didn't know any of them, but they all knew one another. No matter how much they tried to make me feel welcome, I was just a stranger who had walked into their lives and dropped a bombshell.

Sean tried his best to put me totally at ease, though. I felt very relaxed in his company and very grateful to have met him at all. I spent much of that time filling him in on my life and experiences. Like most people, he was shocked. He brought me to the house where he was born, which was now lying derelict, and he also showed me where my birth mother came from and the County Home where I was born. That was the first time I had seen this eerie-looking place and a shiver went down my spine as I stared at the grey building where I drew my first breath.

On one of the days we headed off to find a long-time friend of my foster mother's called Paddy. This man had been her one and only friend for as long as I can remember, stretching back to when I was a young girl, so he knew a lot about my past. I had hoped that he could fill in some of the gaps for me and he was very welcoming and helpful. Some of the things that Paddy told us shocked my brother. He also confirmed a few things that I already knew, such as the abuse and the beatings.

Later that same day I took my brother to meet my foster mother, having previously warned him about her cutting tongue. The meeting went okay, but she was very shocked to see him standing there at her door with me. I believe that she thought I would never succeed in finding anyone connected to me and that I would have given up the chase a long time ago. I think this meeting finally made her realise then how strong a person I actually was, despite everything I had been through.

I felt very much in control that day, more confident in her presence than ever, because for once in my life I had someone standing in that house who was on my side, supporting me. She didn't give me any more information, nor did she want to know anything that I had found, so I decided not to push it. As far as I was concerned that day I had made my point. I had moved on. And I had succeeded in doing it all on my own.

I felt very confident walking away from that house for the first time ever and in a strange way I think I left a lot of my demons behind.

That was the last time I was to see my foster mother. She died a few years later, all alone in a nursing home. This nursing home just happened to be the old County Home, the very same place where I was born all those years ago. It had been converted to a nursing home a decade or so after my birth.

I got a call from a friend to tell me she had died but I didn't attend her funeral. My relationship with my mother was not a good one and I knew my presence would not have been missed.

* * *

I know my search did not lead to me to the ecstatic homecoming that I had expected for over thirty years and I know I never got to meet my father, but I did find some inner peace. I will always be glad that I found my half-brother and that I had the opportunity to meet so many of my father's relatives.

One man whom I was introduced to, my dad's brother, was a former garda. It was then I realised, in a moment of revelation, that this man standing before me was the man outside the pub many years ago who had called me Áine and asked how I was keeping. He never said it was him, but I knew.

It may sound odd but although I was happy that things were finally falling into place I was also very hurt knowing that everyone in my dad's family had known about me – where I was, who I lived with. As I met all these people I felt so alone and regretted that I hadn't asked any of my own children to come with me for support. I was alone, embarrassed and most of all I felt guilty.

Now that I had finally found my family I didn't know what to do next. All my life I had been on my own – I knew it and I felt it. I always felt the odd one out; no matter how hard I tried to belong it never seemed to work. I always did my own thing, as I never had a role model to direct me or advise me. I had also always wondered if I looked like my mother or my father, and if I acted like either of them. Now, through virtual strangers, I knew that I was in fact very like my father, both in looks and mannerisms, and after meeting my mother I was so thankful for that.

Even though my trip back home had opened and released most of the unknown secrets in my own personal Pandora's box, I have to admit that when I left my brother's house that last day I left with a feeling of envy. Envy because he knew our father and I didn't. The knowledge he had of our dad and the memories he possesses are priceless and unfortunately something that I can never have. You cannot buy memories, especially if they are good ones.

Sometimes I wish I could erase all the childhood memories from my own brain and pretend that I came to life when I was twenty-one; then I could just act as though none of this madness ever happened. To this day I am still envious of my brother, although I try my hardest not to be, simply because I now know that he was loved so much as a child, whereas I was just hated. His life was happy, whereas my life was intolerable.

But then I have to ask myself this question: would I be the person I am today if I hadn't lived the life I did? Who knows? What I do know, however, is that I have finally come to accept who I am and what I am. I am now proud to be me, a very unique me.

* * *

In 2002 I stood tall (well, as tall as I could in my five-foot, two-inch frame) and very, very proud when my two daughters graduated from university. I also felt a little sad because their father was not there to see how much they had achieved against all odds.

However, I have talked about this with my children and they agreed that they would not have been able to go to university if their father was still alive, simply because living with alcoholism was, most of the time, impossible mentally, emotionally and financially. They were always worried over how I would cope if they weren't around to support me and they would not have been able to study in our home with all the anxiety and worry.

We have often thought that he died to set us free.

Going to university was something that I never thought was possible, as we struggled so much financially during their three-year courses. I am so very proud of them both and also of my son for all that they have endured in their life and for never ever asking me "Why?" They simply accepted what life had given them and got on with it.

ANN KENNY

Since Liam died I have often thought about alcoholism and the effects it has on a family when the alcoholic dies. I have seen my children go through so much pain and despair in trying to come to terms with their father's death. The sad thing was that I could do nothing for them except be there for them if and when they needed me and I always will.

I have always been terrified that the pain of all I went through would turn me into a bitter and angry person, unable to cope with life. But in time, with the help of my counsellor and Al-Anon, I learned how to let go (most of the time) of the angry feelings that I have around my upbringing – especially around my birth mother and my foster mother.

I knew the moment I left my birth mother's house that day that I would never see or hear from her again, and I haven't. After I discovered that she had given me away, I wondered if I had ever been baptised and if so where it took place and who were my godparents. I decided to write to the parish priest in the town my mother came from and ask him if there were any records of the event. In reply, he sent me a copy of my baptismal certificate, which states that I was baptised on the 12th of August, two days after I was born.

Also in the envelope with the baptismal certificate was a handwritten note from the priest saying, "I note from the Register that you were baptised privately because of serious danger to your health after birth." I was totally shocked by this discovery; if it was me, and my newborn was at risk of dying, no matter what the circumstances, I would want to spend every single moment with her. But obviously not everyone thinks like that. I just wish I knew what had really happened; what illness made me so weak as to require a private baptism?

I also discovered that the name my mother had given me, Anastasia, was not just a lovely name that had popped into her head during the nine months she carried me in her womb. Not at all; it was in fact the name of my brother's mother – my father's wife. And I believe she gave me that name to get at my father and his wife because he had walked away from my mother in her time of need. I have also since learnt that, after she disowned me, she told everyone who knew about her plight that I had died at birth.

I have never been able to find out about the first two years of my life – where I was or who I was with – and there are no medical records of me being ill at birth.

In 2006 I wrote to the Irish government under the Freedom of Information Act asking some questions, such as: Who was Mary Dooley? Were there any medical records of my illness at birth? Who returned me to the County Home? And who signed the papers for my fostering? They were not able to answer any of my questions.

It was then that I realised that I had come to the end of the road in my search for my past and that I must now just let it all go and get on with the rest of my life. However, I have to say that I will never regret going down that road, even though it was painful at times. For me it has been a lifetime experience, to say the least, but not a life-changing one.

POSTSCRIPT

Writing this book has been such a healing process for me. At times it was very painful to recall things from my past. I often disassociated myself from the person I was writing about. Therefore putting it down on paper has been very therapeutic and I can honestly say that I now feel that I have laid most of my demons to rest.

I am still in contact with my brother. However, I have found it very difficult to build a relationship with him. I had become so used to being on my own and having this idea that it was "me against the rest of the world". So when I found this lovely man, someone who actually wanted to be in my life for a change, I didn't know what to do. So I backed away. I couldn't handle it at times that someone really seemed to care for me as a sister and a person, and it was hard for me to believe that he genuinely wanted to get to know me, wanted me to be a part of his life.

However, at that time even I didn't know "me" and I most definitely didn't like who I was. I was ashamed of me – I know now that I shouldn't have been, but I was. I had nothing to show for my fifty-odd years on this planet except my three beautiful children. I had no mansion on a hill or grand clothes to wear. The only thing I had was my five-foot, two-inch frame and a stubborn, defiant attitude to life that has held me in good stead.

Thankfully, my life now is so much different. My children are all very happy and I am so very proud of them. They too have had to deal with so much pain. Watching their mother suffer all those years could not have done them any good. I am now the proud grandmother of an adorable little grandson. He is one of the best things that has ever happened to our family.

I have also finally found true love. Three years ago I met the most wonderful, caring and considerate man of my dreams, who whisked me off my feet and turned my world around. He treats me like a lady and makes every day seem worthwhile. Not only have I found so much happiness with him, but also within myself. He knows of my past and still he is proud to stand by my side. He is now my rock, the stable force I have craved and longed for all those years. He gets on great with my children and he makes a great grandfather.

Thankfully I have now at last found peace with myself and with life. I started a journey to a place unknown to me and although it didn't turn out as I had hoped I now know it all happened for a reason.

If you were to ask me now, knowing what I now know,

would I do it all again, I would still say, most definitely, "Yes". I once heard a saying that life is not a dress rehearsal, you don't get to do it all again. I would say to anyone who has a void that they feel the need to fill in their lives, to get up, get out there and do whatever it takes to make you happy, to give you inner peace. If you don't do it for yourself, nobody else will.

ME, MYSELF AND I

I saw you today as I walked down the street and
I stepped to one side so that we didn't meet.
I watched you pass by with an air of such grace
And I suddenly felt a tear on my face.
You looked so good, so happy and free
And I wondered then if you remembered me.
The last time I saw you my life was a mess
With such sadness and pain no one would have guessed.
But today I saw you like a bright shining star;
It was then that I knew I had come so far.
You stopped and you looked at a window to see
And what I saw was my reflection looking straight
back at ME.

ACKNOWLEDGEMENTS

There are many people I would like to thank whose help and encouragement was invaluable throughout the process of writing this book. Firstly, I would like to thank my children for "being there". Without you my life would be empty.

To everyone at Poolbeg Press and especially to Brian Langan, my editor. Thank you so much, Brian, for all your help and encouragement, for your belief in me when I could not believe in myself, and for your words of wisdom when the going was tough.

A huge thank you to Yvonne Kinsella in helping me put my diaries into this book. Without you, Yvonne, it would not have been possible. I am so grateful for your kindness, thoughtfulness and consideration, and most of all thank you for the words of encouragement when I could not speak, and for letting me be who I was and who I am – a woman, a friend and a mother. Your friendship is deeply appreciated.

To my great friend Tricia who was there for me all those years ago and is still there for me today. To Sally, for helping me to find Ann.

To Brenda, Maureen and Maggie, thank you for putting up with me. I shall concentrate a lot more now!! To Eddie, a big thanks. And to everyone else – you will know who you are – I thank you all from the bottom of my heart.

And last but not least to my partner. My Rock, My Love. Thank you so much for being there for me, especially with the wine, the chocolates and the tissues, and most of all your love.

Ann Kenny
December 2007

ABOUT THE AUTHORS

Ann Kenny has written this book under a pseudonym to protect her identity and that of her family. She is a 57-year-old mother of three and grandmother of one. She now lives very happily with her new partner in the Home Counties.

Yvonne Kinsella is from Dublin and is married with two children. She has worked as a journalist for more than ten years, writing for a number of newspapers and magazines including *The Sunday World*, *Evening Herald*, *Social & Personal*, *Woman's Way* and, most recently, *The Irish Mirror*. She is also a regular contributor on Newstalk radio. She is currently working full-time as a television producer on Irish TV.